• DISCIPLING YOUNG TEENS •

developing CHRISTIAN VALUES

by Kathy Bence

illustrated by Corbin Hillam

STANDARD PUBLISHING
Cincinnati, Ohio

Third Printing, 1993

Expressing the views of her own heart, the author may express views not entirely consistent with those of the publisher.

Unless otherwise indicated, all Scripture quotations are from the *Holy Bible, New International Version,* copyright © 1973, 1978, 1984 by the International Bible Society. Used by permission of Zondervan Bible Publishers and the International Bible Society.

Copyright ©1990, The STANDARD PUBLISHING Company, Cincinnati, Ohio.
A division of STANDEX INTERNATIONAL Corporation.
Printed in U.S.A.

Contents

	Teacher	Workbook
How Can We Teach Values?	4	
1. Who Am I?	5	29
2. Love Me, Love Me Not	7	33
3. Free to Be Me	9	37
4. Why Should I Care About My Neighbors?	11	41
5. Life Is a-Changin'	12	45
6. What's With Sex Anyway?	14	49
7. Evil in the World	16	53
8. Temptation	17	57
9. Guilt and Forgiveness	19	61
10. Parents: A Love/Hate Relationship	21	65
11. The Problem of Money	23	69
12. Fearing the Future	25	73
13. Daily Time Alone With God	26	77

How Can We Teach Values?

"What is right and what is wrong? How do I decide? Who can tell me?"

These are the questions teens are asking today.

"How can we teach values? How do we influence teens with biblical principles?"

These are the questions ministers and parents are asking today.

The series you are about to begin will help to answer values questions for teens as well as provide help for those who wish to influence teens in biblical values development. It resulted from an attempt to disciple my own adolescent daughter, Angela (now 14) when I realized that her values left much to be desired.

I discovered that she sadly lacked information upon which to adopt values. Her self-concept depended on what her mood her best friend was in and what she had said to Angela. Her views on money resulted from what "everyone else" (those hated words) had to spend. Her sense of guilt and conscience development likewise depended on her peers. And all this from a child who had attended church from the age of two weeks!

One evening while attending a curriculum writers' conference, I got the idea for a discipling program for adolescent teens. Originally I thought in terms of mothers discipling their adolescent daughters in biblical thought patterns. Now the series has evolved into a multi-purpose study to be used by an individual teen, a parent, or a youth group at church.

The topics addressed are by no means exhaustive. They represent the issues I heard adolescent girls discussing and those I wanted my daughter to adopt into her value system.

Values are not equivalent to rules. Values are not enforceable. Values are ideas about right and wrong that are chosen because they make sense to the individual. For instance, I am a pacifist. No one has made me so. It is a belief born of my own reflections. I believe it is biblical, just, and the only way I can live with my conscience. Adopting this value produces major effects on my life. I am not free to kill or support any political candidate who supports abortion or war.

Money is a values question for most Christians. How we use our money is a major influence on our lifestyle. I have chosen to live as simple a lifestyle as I can in order to give money to others in the world who have so little. This affects my thinking, my tithing, and my spending.

These types of values patterns are usually adopted as teenagers. The patterns are rarely changed in later years unless values teaching interrupts the process of "peer pressure thinking" (or maybe I should say, "lack of thinking").

Ask your children or your youth group what they think on some of these issues and just see what they say. You may be in for a shock! Try confronting them with some biblical thinking and see if it doesn't make sense to them!

The lessons have been constructed simply enough for adolescents to use this study guide alone. Little instruction should be needed by teachers.

1. Do whatever it takes to make these sessions a discussion, not a lecture. Teens will talk when they feel free of recrimination for saying what they think.

2. Remember, changing of values is a process. Don't expect teens to adopt a complete change of thinking on any issue in one session. Your job is to challenge them on the incompleteness of the typical world view. (If you will emphasize the fairness of God's ways, it will appeal to teens more.)

3. Make sure that what you say is true of your own life and value system.

4. Remember that values are principles to apply to a variety of experiences. Try not to make rules out of biblical ideas. In the end, God must work His thinking into teens. We must challenge. He will transform.

Kathy Bence
June 1989

LESSON 1

Who Am I?

Lesson Goals
To set in place the following foundational truths (upon which subsequent lessons build):
• Who God is
• Who human beings are
• The possibility of God/person interaction and relationship

Introduction

As young minds mature, they begin to grapple with the basic questions all thinking people struggle with. For young teens, matters of personal identity—"Who am I? What makes me unique? What traits do I share with all people?"—take on new importance. Childish concepts of God lose their adequacy, and a new quest for knowledge of God arises.

Even adult Christians, who have their faith in place, find these questions continually appearing in new form. Our discovery of ever-fresh answers stimulates further growth.

Adolescents are struggling with these questions for the first time. Pat answers won't help them. They move toward understanding, but at their own pace. Youth leaders can help them by lovingly seeking to understand them and guide them toward biblical truth.

Teacher Tips

1. Establish a pattern of free communication. Risk personal vulnerability by relating your own struggles (past or present) to understand these truths.

To help your students feel free to share their struggles, they need to know that you too have faced (and do face) the pressures of life. Try sharing a painful experience from your life—a serious illness, the death of someone close to you—that reminded you how small you were and how distant God seemed.

2. Sense the mood of your teens. Particularly if they seem open from the beginning, give them opportunity to share experiences of their own (either pleasant, as in the lesson introduction, or painful, following your example) that forced them to ask questions foundational to life itself.

3. Try to draw in those who remain silent by calling on them by name and asking them a question.

4. Make use of visual appeal by using a chalkboard to list answers to Questions 1, 6, 12, 14, and 15.

Have your students read Genesis 1 either silently or aloud. Then lead them in a discussion based on the questions in their lessons.

Answers

1. The very first verse of the Bible describes God in terms of two basic facts. What are they?
a. God existed before the world, in the beginning.
b. God created the world.

2. Genesis 1 does not give us any proof that God exists or explain how He began. What reasons can you think of why it does not do this?
There is no absolute proof for God's existence. The Bible never argues for the existence of God. His presence is assumed authoritatively. However, Genesis 1 offers the world itself as primary evidence of God's existence. You might point out to the students that the world does exist. They must either believe that someone (a being such as God) planned and formed it, or that it happened by mere chance. They must decide which makes more sense.

Man knows little or nothing about God's existence or action before the creation of the world.

3. What does your answer to Question 2 tell you about who you are and how you can know God? How long do you think people have been asking these questions?
These basic questions are not new. People throughout history have struggled with these issues. The fact that everyone asks the same questions indicates a higher being, or creator.

4. What does Genesis 1 tell you about *how* God created our world?
He spoke and the world came into being.

5. If God could create out of nothing, what one trait must He possess?
Infinite power or strength.

**6. Note the order in which God created. Briefly

5

list God's "projects" during the first six days.
Day 1: heavens and earth, light and darkness
Day 2: sky
Day 3: land and sea, plants
Day 4: sun, moon, stars
Day 5: birds and sea creatures
Day 6: land animals, man, and woman

7. Could God have reversed that order? What seems right about the sequence God chose?

We do not understand the order of creation completely. For example, light was created before the sun, moon, and stars. It is possible that in the first days, God himself was the light, as He will be in the last days (see Revelation 22:5). Yet, the basic sequence of creation appears logical. To thrive, the plants needed the previously created light, dry land, and water. Animals (including man) needed those same conditions, as well as plants for food.

8. The way God planned His creation lets you see that, from the beginning, God was a _____ God.

Wise

9. God cared enough about the living things He created to give them the resources they needed. This gives you a hint of God's _____.

Love

10. Does the thought of this huge God, as seen in Genesis 1, comfort you or frighten you? Why do you feel that way?

Your students will likely respond with the expected answer—comfort. Allow them the opportunity to express the comfort they find in their picture of God, particularly His love.

Encourage them also to explore the fear-inspiring nature of God. A God of His infinite power is not merely a pal to be toyed with.

11. Based on what you've learned so far, do you think God is an "it" or a person?

God is a person. But go on to explore the reasoning behind this answer. They have described a God who creates, knows, and loves. Non-living objects cannot do any of these three. God must be a person.

12. What one thing does God do in verses 3, 6, 9, 11, 14, 20, 24, 26, 28, and 29? What does this tell you about what God can do with you?

God speaks; He is able to express himself and communicate with people. God can tell us who He is, who we are, and what we should do.

13. What do the answers to questions 11 and 12 tell you about the possibility of your knowing God?

Nonliving objects cannot participate in relationships. People cannot relate with chairs or stones. God is not a "thing" or a "force." He is a living person with whom we can interact.

14. According to Genesis 1, what made men and women special compared to the rest of God's creation? In other words, what two special features did God plan for human beings (v. 1:26)?

a. Men and women were created in God's image.
b. They were to have dominion (limited control) over the other creations in the visible world.

15. If you were created in God's image, then what divine traits (ones you have already listed that relate to God) must *you* possess?

Power, wisdom, love, personhood, and the ability to communicate.

16. Does Genesis 1 tell you of anything else God created in His image? What does this tell you about yourself? About the possibility of knowing God?

Persons are the only part of creation God made in His own image. This tells us that we are important. God gave human beings a position of unique honor. Our likeness to God enables us to know Him and be like Him as no other part of creation can.

Wrap-up

Give your students a piece of paper on which to list all they know about God based on this one chapter of the Bible. Or you may wish to list these characteristics on the chalkboard (see Summary, p. 32). Then ask each student to share one fact he has learned about God that is most meaningful to him and tell why it is meaningful.

Close by giving thanks that God knows us and desires to communicate with us.

Prayer: Lord God, you know who you made me to be. Help me to be true to your vision of "the real me." In Jesus' name, amen.

LESSON 2

Love Me, Love Me Not

Lesson Goals
• To help teens base their self-acceptance on God's acceptance of them
• To enable teens to grasp the value of uniqueness
• To encourage teens to live according to God's image of them—precious and unique

Introduction

This study highlights what you already know: that many of your teens are struggling with their lack of feelings of self-worth. They're just beginning to see themselves as unfinished products. Sometimes they like what they see. More often, their weaknesses overwhelm them. When they compare themselves with others around them. it heightens this negative view of themselves. The media, with its presentation of "perfect 10's," makes them despair.

It may bring out strange behavior as they try to cover their lack of love for themselves by loud talk, mocking, or contempt for today's topic.

Teacher Tips

Today's lesson, if it is to be effective, must be approached openly and honestly by you the teacher.

You may want to begin today's session by sharing something about yourself you've never liked or fully accepted (or how God has helped you accept it).

With this openness, others will feel freer to admit frustration rather than covering it with rude behavior.

To help teens accept themselves:

1. Teach them to celebrate, rather than mourn, their own uniqueness.
2. Suggest that they make Jesus the hero of their lives, rather than TV stars.
3. Remind them that Jesus loves and uses unique individuals.

Answers

If you could instantly change three things about yourself, what would they be? I would like to be
(taller, smarter, athletic, outgoing, popular, older, a leader, thinner, better-looking, spiritual)

Read Genesis 1:26, 27 to get a better understanding of how God made us.

1. From the beginning, God decided that people shouldn't all be exactly alike. What do you see in these verses to support that statement? Why didn't God make everyone the same?
It was necessary, in order for God to make the human race in His own image, to place different bits of himself in a variety of people. No single person could contain the entire divine image.

2. As different as persons are, they all possess one common feature. What is it? Why is this common feature so important?
God created *all* persons in His own image. No matter who we are, what we're like, or what we think of ourselves, we all possess a basic similarity to God. This God-likeness gives value to us all.

3. Thousands of years after God created men and women, He chose to come down to earth and become a person like them. What does this tell you of God's opinion of persons in general?
Even though mankind had strayed from God, He still saw value in His original idea (man as he could be) and hoped for a restoration (God could remake him). God values persons!

4. As Jesus was showing the world what God is like, He could have chosen several different methods. Jesus sometimes spoke to large crowds, but He spent most of His time with twelve men. How many of the disciples can you list by name? (see Mark 3:16-19)

5. With the help of the appropriate Bible verses, link each disciple with the words best describing him.
a. *Philip* sometimes seemed a little bit slow (John 6:5, 12:21, 14:8).
b. *John* was probably a quiet sort, unless something aroused his temper (Mark 9:38, Luke 9:54, John 13:23, 20:21-24).

7

c. *Thomas* was a hard-nosed guy, perhaps with a scientific mind; he would believe only what he could see (John 11:16, 20:25).

d. *James, son of Zebedee* still let his mom speak for him, even as an adult (Matthew 20:20, 21).

e. *Judas* betrayed Jesus (Matthew 26:47-49).

f. *Simon Peter* was a good leader, but sometimes put his foot in his mouth (Matthew 16:16, 22).

g. *Simon the Zealot* was a political activist (Acts 1:13).

h. *Nathaniel (Bartholomew)* was quick to decide, sometimes a good trait and sometimes not (John 1:46-49).

i. *James, son of Alphaeus* was unknown; the Bible tells us only his father's name (Acts 1:13).

j. *Thaddeus (Judas)* must have been a quiet man; all we know is that he asked one question (John 14:22).

k. *Andrew* lived in the shadow of his brother, yet brought people to Jesus (John 1:40, 6:8).

l. *Matthew* had not been the most respectable guy before he met Jesus (Matthew 9:9, 11).

6. For each of the following sentences, circle the word that is true.

a. The disciples were all quite *different*.

b. The disciples *did not* always follow Jesus well.

c. The Bible *does not* tell a lot about each disciple.

7. Why did Jesus choose disciples who were so different from each other and from Him?

Jesus had no choice but to choose imperfect people. But each of these twelve different people could serve Him. Each had a unique set of strengths and weaknesses.

8. Based on your answers to the last two questions, what do you think about each of the following statements?

a. Jesus loves one type of person (maybe the smart or the beautiful) more than the rest.

It appears that Jesus did not choose the twelve most brilliant, most handsome, or most anything persons. He chose men who varied greatly from each other. Jesus must love all types of people.

b. Jesus chooses only those who do everything right to be His followers.

Jesus chose as disciples men who had been (and would be) far from perfect. Jesus' offer of love remains unchanged. We do not have to earn His love.

c. Those who stand out in the crowd are more important to God than "ordinary" people.

Jesus chose disciples who appear quite average. He did not select the twelve best candidates for "Mr. Israel." Jesus loves ordinary people.

9. Mark 3:13-15 show us Jesus as He was choosing the twelve disciples. What does it tell us about how He felt toward them?

He wanted them *to be with Him*. Jesus has not changed. In many ways He can help you improve as a person, but even now, He loves you as you are.

When you are feeling down about yourself, it's often because you're comparing yourself to someone you think is better than you. Even Jesus' disciples fell into this habit (see Mark 9:33, 34 and Luke 22:24).

10. Verse 13 says Jesus called to himself "those whom He wanted." Why do you think Jesus wants *you* to be with Him?

11. Check below those statements that enable you to better accept yourself *just as you are right now*:

- God made me who I am
- God made me for a purpose
- Jesus wants me to be with Him
- I am special because I am uniquely made
- I don't have to be like anyone else
- God accepts me as I am, with all my "warts"
- I don't have to be perfect to be loved

12. How is your thinking about yourself changed by the knowledge that God accepts you?

Wrap-up

Emphasize that God loves your students just as they are. However, they need to love and accept themselves. To help them do this, ask them to complete the following sentences.

1. One thing I really like about the way God made me is:

2. My greatest strength (character trait, *not* a skill) is:

3. One way I can serve God is:

Close by giving thanks that God made us the way we are and that He accepts us. We do not need to earn His love.

Prayer: Lord God, I want to like myself but I need your help. Please show me that you love me first. In Jesus' name, amen.

LESSON 3

Free to Be Me

Lesson Goals
• To enable teens to make choices they can live with.
• To help teens realize that choices are based on our values.
• To encourage teens to make choices based on biblical principles (as opposed to society's values).

Introduction

Making choices may be one of the most critical and least addressed topics for teens today. The ability to make wise decisions in the face of pressure is a skill we use all our lives. But upon what basis do we make decisions—whim, peer pressure, or biblical principles?

Today's lesson focuses on Joseph's decision-making processes and ours. Emphasize the results of our choices. Freedom to make choices automatically means taking responsibility for the consequences.

Encourage your students to make decisions independent of peer pressure and take a stand for what they believe in.

Teacher Tips

To bring this lesson home:
1. Emphasize this tension between their own desires and the influences (for good and bad) around them.
2. Suggest that they adopt biblical principles as their standards of right and wrong (see answers to Question 9).
3. Point out that the world's choices are usually based on looking out for #1.
4. Remind them that their self-image is based on God's acceptance (refer back to Lesson 2), so they are free from peer pressure (approval) to choose according to God's standards. (If we have God's approval, we no longer need the approval of other people.)

You know your students' Bible knowledge. Based on that, choose the best means for refreshing their memory of the Joseph story. Reading the entire story would take too long. Either retell it in your own words or have the students tell it to each other (perhaps you could choose small groups within the class have read assigned portions of the Scripture).

You'll want to read Genesis 37 and 39 again to refresh yourself with these incidents in Joseph's life so you can tell the story rather than read it.

List daily choices (from Question 1) and guidelines for decision-making (Question 9) on the chalkboard.

Answers

1. How does this gift of power reflect God's image in Adam and Eve?

In creating the world, God displayed His power. After the creation of Adam and Eve, God delegated part of His power to them. As He ruled the universe, they would rule the plant and animal life around them. Just as God makes decisions, He gives humans the ability to make conscious choices. This ability separates persons from other forms of life.

2. What limits did God place on Adam and Eve's power?

The only explicit limit involved the tree of knowledge of good and evil. Of course, the basic assumption behind God's commands was His overall rule.

3. Within these limits, did Adam and Eve still possess great freedom? What types of choices remained open to them?

Within their ideal environment, Adam and Eve could do almost anything they pleased. They could choose to work, play, or rest. In each other, God, and even the animals, they had friends to enjoy. There were few limits to their pleasure and self-development.

Examine each of the following incidents in Joseph's life in terms of Questions 4-7.

a. His dreams (Genesis 37:3-11)
b. Sold into slavery (Genesis 37:25-28, 39:1-4)
c. Potiphar's wife (Genesis 39:5-19)
d. An unjust prison term (Genesis 39:19-23)

Question 7 is the most important of the four. Use that question as your "goal," shaping discussion so the students will be able to make a sound answer to it.

4. What did the people around Joseph hope (or expect) he would do?
  a. Keep his dreams for the future for himself.
  b. See life as an awful experience; become discouraged and bitter; take out his anger on others.
  c. Yield to sexual temptation.
  d. Similar to (b) above.

5. What did Joseph choose to do?
  a. Tell his dreams to the whole family.
  b. Follow his God; faithfully serve Potiphar.
  c. Flee from temptation.
  d. Follow his God; faithfully serve the prison warden.

6. What happened as a result?
  a. His brothers sold him into slavery.
  b. Potiphar promoted him to a position of honor; God blessed his work.
  c. Potiphar threw him in prison.
  d. The warden promoted him to a position of honor; God blessed his work.

7. Do you feel Joseph made the best decision? Why?
  a. Probably not. His dreams did later come true, but bragging about his future served no good purpose at that time.
  b. Yes. Moaning and groaning about life's miseries would merely have made everyone miserable. Life gave Joseph lemons, and he made lemonade!
  c. Yes. Had he given in, he would have taken that which was not his, betraying both Potiphar and God.
  d. Similar to (b) above.

8. In each of the four situations, Joseph chose not to conform to what others expected of him. Is this always the best decision? Why?
No. For example, Joseph followed his own wishes in telling the family about the dreams, and ended up in a hole (literally). Our own ideas are not always best. Often others know better than we do.

9. What guidelines can you adopt to help you make decisions?
  Before I decide, I can _____.
  To help me weigh the options, I should _____.
  If I have doubts, I _____.
  To keep me from messing up, I should _____.

This question has no complete list of right and wrong answers. Within reason, allow free discussion here. You might want to list on a chalkboard those principles the entire group adopts. Some possibilities include:

  1. God is the ultimate ruler. We should submit to Him (see Question 2 above).
  2. God has communicated His guidelines with us. When in doubt, see what the Bible recommends. (The first examples of this occur in Genesis 1:28-30. He later gave other commands, preserved for us in Scripture.)
  3. Consider the long-term results. Which would have made Joseph happier—to accept his mistreatment and go on to make life as pleasant as possible, or to sit around and complain? Which moved him ahead?
  4. Don't always choose the easiest route. Be willing to pay a price to do what is right (as Joseph did concerning Potiphar's wife.)
  5. Don't let circumstances rule you. You can do what is best even when life has given you a bad turn.
  6. When others in authority over you make decisions for you, it is generally to your advantage to follow them (the tree of knowledge).
  7. When in doubt, don't. Doubts are warnings to us to reconsider.
  8. Never make a choice because someone pressures you to conform. Act like the unique individual God created.
  9. Pray. God will guide you if you ask.

10. List three steps in the decision-making process.

11. Apply these three steps to a decision you are considering right now in your life.

Wrap-up

Challenge your group to become leaders who help others to do right. Suggest that they encourage their friends to defy peer pressure and adopt standards of their own.

Ask them to choose one issue on which they will not only take a stand but encourage others to do right. Ask volunteers to share their issue with the group.

Close with a prayer for courage for individuals as well as loving support among the group.

LESSON 4

Why Should I Care About My Neighbors?

Lesson Goals
• to make teens aware of needs in the world.
• to motivate teens to care about the helpless neighbors around them.
• to help them envision themselves as helpers

Introduction

Young teens do not naturally think in terms of others' needs. They are so caught up in their own physical and emotional changes that they feel needy themselves. Since, time is the answer to their needs, they could stay enmeshed in their own egocentric world till well into their twenties.

However, concern for others is an attitude that can be learned, just like any other. For most people, just seeing the needs of others is sufficient motivation to help. Teens need to be confronted and informed to make them "world-aware." You might want to show a short film or read a magazine article on some hurting group in this country or another country. Use this film or display the pictures to get your students thinking outside their own sphere of operation.

Teaching Tips

Today's discussion is a difficult one to lead if you aren't actively involved in helping others yourself.

1. Share with your group either how you are helping others or how you *should* be helping others (and then resolve to).

2. Try not to label your students as selfish, even if they are not concerned with the needs of others. Remember how small their worlds are—friends, school, appearance.

3. Try not to use guilt in your attempts to motivate them to concern for others. Rather, emphasize that the Good Samaritan chose to help because it was the right thing to do.

4. Come prepared with information on needy neighbors in your area: homeless, disabled, poor, lonely, senior citizens, and single parents, whom they could assist in practical ways.

5. Teens may need your help and encouragement to see how they are capable of helping needy people. Discuss the value of a friend's support in hard times. Then suggest that they be that kind of friend to someone in need.

Answers

1. List your three major concerns in life (in priority order).

2. Where did the needs of others figure into your concerns?

3. Was Cain concerned for his brother's welfare? Should he have been?
Cain wasn't concerned for his brother's welfare, but God's reaction (v. 10) indicates that he should have been.

4. What do you think it means to be "your brother's keeper" (or sister's)?
• feeding/clothing them
• babysitting/odd jobs for friends
• helping the poor and homeless
• loving people as they are
• all of the above

Turn to Luke 10:30-36, the story of the Good Samaritan.

5. List the events that happened to the victim in this story (v. 30).
 a. robbed
 b. stripped of clothes
 c. beaten
 d. left for dead

6. Now imagine that you are the first person to walk by this man. You see the blood and you hear him moan. Write below what your first reaction to this situation would be.

7. Now look at verse 33 to see what the Samaritan did for the victim. List his actions below:
• He bandaged his wounds

11

• He poured oil/wine on wounds (this was used as disinfectant in those days)
• He put the man on his own donkey for traveling
• He took the man to an inn
• He paid the innkeeper for the victim's care
• He promised to pay more if necessary

8. Why do you think the Samaritan went to all this bother for a stranger?
He cared about the man's pain as if it were his own.

9. Verse 29 says that Jesus told this story to answer the question, "Who is my neighbor?" How do you think the victim was the Samaritan's "neighbor?"
A "neighbor" can be any fellow human being.

10. In verse 27 Jesus says we are to love God with all our hearts and love our neighbors as ourselves. Define what it would mean in your life to love one of your "neighbors" as you love yourself.

11. Who are your neighbors?

12. Who among your neighbors (in the broadest sense) is in need of help?

13. Check the types of help they need on this list:
(Food, clothing, friendship, an advocate, money, help with schoolwork, babysitting or odd jobs, a listening ear, an invitation to your house, prayer, an invitation to church)

14. Which of these can you provide for one of your "neighbors" in need?

Wrap-up

To round off this discussion, emphasize Questions 12-14. Give each teen a piece of paper and pen to "brainstorm" on paper for ways they can help a needy neighbor. Encourage them by reassuring them of their value as helpers.

Even 13- or 14-year-olds can offer valuable help as a babysitter for a single mother, visiting a lonely person, or running errands for someone who's ill. Remind them that it doesn't take a lot of money or skill—just concern for the needs of others.

Prayer: Dear God, help me to care about the needs of my neighbors around me. In Jesus' name, amen.

LESSON 5

Life Is a-Changin'

Lesson Goals
• to help teens realize that God is in control of every situation
• to help teens develop trust in an unchanging God as a secure foundation in a world of change

Introduction

Surely we live in the fastest-changing era ever. No one is more aware of this fact than today's teen. They live in a throwaway society. As if that weren't enough, there's the ever-present fear of everything being wiped out with only three minutes warning.

While they may say they like this fast-paced change, most of them are terrified by the uncertainties of life. They long for something or someone constant to hang on to.

This lesson presents God as the only one who never changes, the only one from whom they can expect any security. Use this discussion to create trust in the unchanging God.

Teacher Tips

Today's lesson could evoke strong feelings of discomfort in those teens who feel insecurity. Be alert and sensitive to unusual behavior.

If possible, change the setting of the room where you meet before your teens arrive. Rearrange furniture and make any obvious changes possible. Then wait for someone to mention it. (If no one does, you'll need to mention it.) Explain that change is the topic of today's lesson. Ask if they like the room better as it is or as it was before.

To begin, discuss jointly Question 4 (What thing in their lives is the most dependable) and Question 5

(Does life ever change too quickly for them). Before you look at Isaiah 40, move on to a brief discussion of whether God ever changes.

While looking at Isaiah 40 yourself, note the basic emphases of these three passages:
verses 6-8, man's "wither-ability"
verses 10-14, God's power, yet His tenderness
verses 21-24, 28-31, God's unchanging control of the world and us

These three emphases are vital to communicate to your teens if you are to help them understand God's abiding love and help available to us.

Read this passage several times, meditating on the greatness of God, before you attempt to communicate these concepts to your teens.

Answers

1. How often do you change your:
- hairstyle
- best friend
- weight
- favorite TV show
- church
- favorite teacher
- posters on your wall
- girl- or boyfriend
- bedtime
- style of dress
- favorite sport
- makeup
- ideas of right and wrong

2. List five things in your life that you never intend to change.

3. What aspects of your life would you most like to change?

4. What one thing (or person) in your life do you consider the most dependable?

5. Do you ever feel that life changes too fast?
Often   Sometimes   Never

6. Do you think God ever changes?
Yes   No   Not sure

7. Look at the contrast in these verses and complete the following thoughts to make them true (according to Isaiah 40:6-8).
Humanity will not last forever; God's Word will last forever.

8. What adjective in the following list best describes God as found in Isaiah 40:10?
Powerful, interested

9. What do the sheep (flock) represent in verse 11? How does it make you feel to think of God carrying you in His arms?
Us, His children; safe

10. What impression do verses 12, 13 give you of God?
Although God is all-powerful, He is also all loving.

11. List the amazing things God is able to do from the following verses:
v. 22: sits high over the earth; bigger than people
v. 23: controls rulers of the world
v. 24: same as 23
v. 28: creator of the earth
v. 28: lasts forever
v. 29: gives strength to weary people
      unlimited understanding/knowledge

12. What impression do these verses give you of God?

13. Now list the ways He can help *you*.
v. 29: gives strength when I'm weary
      increases my power when I'm weak
v. 31: renews my strength
      makes me soar like eagles
      I can run but not get weary
      I can walk but not faint

14. Now, thinking about the change and uncertainty in your life, consider what it means to have this powerful, unchanging God to help you. Write below one way God can help you face the uncertainty that most scares you.
God can give you strength to "soar" over the problem of:

Wrap-up

To conclude this discussion, let teens help you return the room to its normal state. (This provides the emotional satisfaction of "visible" society). Then ask everyone to quietly consider Question 14, which shows that God is a source of security for our lives.

Ask if anyone would like to share a new insight or a concern for prayer. Then close with a shared prayer session, centering around God as our security in the "changingness" of life. (Try prayer in pairs to avoid shyness in praying in front of a group.)

Prayer: Thank You, dear God, that though everything else in life may change, you will always be there for me. In Jesus' name, amen.

LESSON 6

What's With Sex Anyway?

Lesson Goals
• to help teens consider sex objectively in light of consequences of its misuse
• determine to obey God's injunctions against sex outside marriage.

Introduction

A bit of history on the Bathsheba episode may prove helpful for answering questions.

People in those days had houses constructed with flat roofs. These roofs were used as porches, especially in the evening. People even slept there to escape the heat. Households were large and privacy for bathing rare.

Bathsheba may or may not have known that King David was watching, but she certainly would have known he lived nearby. She would have had little choice in obeying a royal command to sleep with the king.

None of these conditions make their sin any less serious, but help to place it in a cultural context that helps us understand the story.

This lesson will elicit highly charged emotions and opinions. Again, they will probably regard God as mean to restrict a natural urge that He himself gave us. Remember, however, that teens feel compelled to rebel against something. If it weren't a restriction on sex, it would be something else.

Teacher Tips

This lesson will be less difficult if you can relax and feel comfortable about discussing sex. Think of it as God's gift and a priority of God's to teach teens proper use of this gift.

Try to keep the discussion off the people present and speak in terms of sex in general (not "what's OK for me," but "what God thinks about sex"). This will ward off some embarrassment and also rebellion against biblical injunctions against sex.

Try to emphasize the dire results in David and Bathsheba's affair. David's ministry was never the same again. Nor was his relationship with God ever as close afterwards. Our sin *matters* to God—He loves us and cares whether we are happy or miserable, so He makes rules and guidelines for us to live by. If we live by His rules we will live happier lives than when we go our own way. Following God does not bring us misery, but joy and blessing.

Answers

True or False

T   God created sex, so He knows best how it should be used
F   Sex is OK between two people who love each other, married or not
F   God is mean to restrict intercourse to marriage
F   Sex is God's gift, so we can use it any way we choose
F   Sex is strictly a physical act, with no life-changing effects
F   I must look and act sexy if I don't want to be left out
T   To husbands and wives, sex is a beautiful means of communication
F   Sex is necessary to hold on to a boyfriend or girlfriend
F   The church is out of touch to forbid sex outside of marriage
T   Sex includes mind, body, and emotions; it is most meaningful in a lasting relationship
F   Decisions about sex should be left to each individual
T   The Bible's view of sex presents it as good, and best if kept for marriage

Genesis 2:20-25 implies that Adam wasn't happy even in this perfect environment. What emotion do you think Adam was experiencing?
Loneliness

1. What sort of role was Eve created to fulfill in Adam's life?
Companion, wife, lover (all three)

2. Verse 22 says God made Eve by taking out one of Adam's ribs. What sort of relationship did

God intend Adam and Eve to have?
Unity/oneness

3. When Adam exclaimed about Eve, "Bone of my bone and flesh of my flesh!" (v. 23), what emotion do you think Adam felt toward Eve?
Joy/excitement/love

4. Verse 24 says that man and woman will leave their parents to live together. What kind of relationship does this imply? What does the word "cleave" mean?
Permanent; stick together/become one emotionally

5. Why do you think verse 26 was included in the Bible?
To show that nakedness between two people God has placed together is good and right.

6. God obviously intended sex to be a part of male/female relationships, but why do you suppose He restricted it to marriage?
It is most meaningful between two people God has placed together is good and right.

Now read 2 Samuel 11.

7. What was wrong with David watching a beautiful woman take a bath?
David placed himself in a position to make temptation difficult to resist.

8. What could Bathsheba have done to avoid exciting David?
She could have bathed where no one could see her.

9. Put the events of the story in the proper order.
  (7) a. Bathsheba gets pregnant
  (1) b. Bathsheba bathes on rooftop at night
  (4) c. David sends for Bathsheba
  (2) d. David sees Bathsheba bathing
  (5) e. Bathsheba comes to David
  (3) f. David lusts for Bathsheba
  (6) g. David seduces Bathsheba

10. Write below what David and Bathsheba could have done next.

What did David, king of Israel, choose to do?

11. Verse 17 tells us that Uriah, Bathsheba's husband, did die in battle. How do you think David and Bathsheba felt?
Guilty (they may say relieved)

12. After that, Bathsheba mourned Uriah (it was custom), moved into David's house, and had a baby boy. What word describes the Lord's reaction to this?
Displeased

13. The Lord was so displeased that He caused the baby to become ill and die (12:15-18). Look at David's reaction in verse 16. List what David did.
• wept
• fasted
• prayed/pleaded with God to let the child live
• spent his nights lying on the ground

14. Do you think David thought seducing Bathsheba worth killing her husband and their baby?
No

15. What conclusions do you draw from this story about the results of misusing sex?

16. Could it be that God *knows* that misusing sex causes pain for us? List below three ways misusing sex can cause misery for you.

Wrap-up

Give your teens a piece of paper and suggest they draw up several guidelines to the proper use of sex for their own lives.

First, ask them to do this individually. Then suggest they gather in small groups to discuss their guidelines. (Omit if you think the atmosphere too charged or the teens too shy to discuss sex openly.)

Close with a prayer for the strength to resist the temptation to follow the world's views; rather to obey God's wishes concerning sex.

Prayer: Dear God, help me to trust that when You say "no" that You know best. In Jesus' name, amen.

LESSON 7

Evil in the World

Lesson Goals
• to help teens understand where evil in the world originated.
• to enable teens to see good and evil as a battle in which they must daily choose sides.
• to encourage them to trust God's wisdom in giving us a plan for living (via His commands).

Introduction

Although this same passage was used in Lesson 7, the emphasis differs in that the focus of the lesson is temptation, centering around Eve. Lesson 8 focuses on the origin of evil (serpent/Satan) and its effects on us as we try to obey God.

Teens are well aware of the evil in life, yet they may not have understood how it came to be a part of life. This lesson could be a critical one in helping your teens live a consistent Christian walk.

Begin today's lesson by asking teens to recall their earliest memory of doing wrong. Then ask why they could do wrong at such an early age. Allow for their answers. Then ask: Where did this inclination in a child to do wrong come from?

Teacher Tips

Today's lesson could become a sticky one if you allow the discussion to be sidetracked. Try to avoid:
• discussing why God doesn't stop all evil (no one can understand His timing and purposes for life)
• setting up a hierarchy of sins (all sins are equal because all are disobedience to God)
• getting off onto side issues or specific sins
• any mockery or derision if anyone shares

Make the discussion as easy for them as you can by taking their comments seriously (even though some of them may have some wrong ideas).

Because someone is bound to ask, the Bible does tell us that Satan is a fallen angel who set himself against God and was then thrown out of Heaven. Here on earth, he thus sets himself up against good and tries to win converts to evil. Satan will not always reign on earth. Revelation 20:10 tells us that God will destroy him in the end and reign victorious forever.

Answers

1. Which of the following choices do you think best depicts evil? (abortion, war, starving nations, murder/crime, selfishness, hating God, disease)

2. On a scale of 1 to 10 (10 = highest), rate these results of evil as they affect *your* life (How much do you suffer because of _____?)

• abortion	1	2	3	4	5	6	7	8	9	10
• war	1	2	3	4	5	6	7	8	9	10
• starving nations	1	2	3	4	5	6	7	8	9	10
• murder/crime	1	2	3	4	5	6	7	8	9	10
• selfishness	1	2	3	4	5	6	7	8	9	10
• hating God	1	2	3	4	5	6	7	8	9	10
• disease	1	2	3	4	5	6	7	8	9	10

3. Write why you think there is evil in the world.

4. Compare Genesis 1:31 and 2:25 with 3:7, 8 and 3:23, 24.

1:31 and 2:25	3:7, 8 and 3:23, 24
Life was good (as God made it)	Realizing naked
	Hiding from God
Naked and no shame	Banished from God
Contentment	Couldn't return to garden
	Misery

5. Refer to Genesis 3:1-7 and analyze as follows: Person/What he(she) did/What happened then/What choice was involved

a. Eve/used persuasion/Eve ate fruit/disobey God
b. Serpent/tempted the woman/Eve said no/yield to temptation
c. Adam/accepted fruit/ate it/disobey God

6. Who was evil in the passage?
The serpent

7. What was evil in the passage?
Doing what God had forbidden; the serpent doubting God's command

8. What two words describe the serpent (v. 1)?
Subtle and wild

9. Define what the serpent really meant by the following statements:
When the serpent said, "Did God say, 'You shall not eat of any tree in the garden?'" he really meant, "Surely God won't deny you some measly fruit."
When the serpent said, "You will not die," he really meant, "I know more than God and I say you won't die."

10. What then was evil in the serpent?
Setting himself up as authority over God.
What other name does the Bible use for the serpent?

11. How does evil affect your life? Answer the following questions true or false.
• I get really concerned about starving people.
• If I saw a parent abusing a child, I would try to stop him.
• Evil in the world really doesn't touch my life.
• I would participate in a peace march near my home.
• I don't really get upset when I read the newspapers.
• I believe disease is due to evil in the world.

12. Do you think God meant for the world to be full of evil? Why do you think He allowed the serpent to defile His world?
No; he gave Eve a choice whom to love and serve.

13. List below two or three ways in which you have been choosing your own way over what you know to be God's desires.

14. Write below, in two or three sentences, how you'd like to live your Christian life.

Wrap-up

Focus on Question 13, how they would like to live a Christian life (if they were able to live above evil). God does not tempt us (James 1:13-15); just the opposite, He desires to help us stand against wrong. Encourage your students by emphasizing how much God loves them; He has given them guidelines to live by to make it easier to live a life of righteousness (via the biblical commands).

Prayer: Dear God, please help me to stop and think before I act so I can obey you. In Jesus' name, amen.

LESSON 8

Temptation

Lesson Goals
• to enable teens to understand the origins of temptation.
• to help teens realize that temptation does not equal sin.
• to help teens see the times and places when they've most often been susceptible to temptation.

Introduction

Begin today's lesson with an object lesson. Bring in a plate of pastries or doughnuts. Set them in the center of the room with a "Do Not Touch" sign propped near them, and leave the room until it is time to begin.
Begin by asking, "Was anyone tempted to sneak a doughnut while I wasn't there?"
Discuss what kept them from taking a doughnut despite the sign. Include the comment, "We usually get what we want badly enough, no matter who says no. Temptation is what our discussion today considers."
Share the doughnuts before beginning the lesson.

Teacher Tips

Today's lesson may make some teens uncomfortable. They might feel guilt over sins committed, or they might fear pressure to confess sins before others.
The lesson goals are planned neither to induce guilt or confess it. Try to steer discussion away from specific sins or specific people. Concentrate on temptation in general—its origins, patterns, and results.
Emphasize how Eve yielded for selfish reasons on the spur of the moment. She consulted neither God nor Adam. She acted on impulse, just as Satan hopes we will.
Do all you can to express acceptance of your teens

even with their sins. We are all sinners, saved by grace.

Answers

1. How is the serpent described?
Crafty (or subtle, or cunning, or wily)

2. How do you think the serpent acted craftily toward Eve?
He knew her weak spot and exploited her desire to be like God.

3. How did Eve prove she knew what God expected of her (vv. 2, 3)?
Eve obviously knew God's wishes because she quoted them to Satan.

4. With what appeal did Satan tempt Eve (vv. 4, 5)?
Satan appealed to Eve's desire to be like (as great as) God.

5. What were Eve's choices for response in this situation?
Eve's responses might have included running away, stopping to think the situation through, or instant obedience to God's command.

6. Why do you think God allowed Eve a choice (temptation)?
God allowed Eve a choice because He made us thinking creatures, not puppets.

7. What three things helped Eve give in to temptation (v. 6)?
Eve saw that the fruit was good to eat, she liked the way it looked, and she wanted the wisdom she could gain by eating it.

8. Describe an ad or commercial you've seen that is based on:
- **food appeal**
- **eye appeal**
- **promises that you'll be thought intelligent, sexy, or "with it"**

Did it sell you on their product?

Did these ads use Christian or nonChristian principles to sell their product?

9. What two things did Eve stand to lose by eating the fruit?
By eating the fruit, Eve would lose her innocence and her perfect relationship with God.

10. Why do you think Eve couldn't be satisfied with some fruit from another tree that was allowed?
Eve couldn't be satisfied as long as anything was forbidden to her. She wanted total freedom without responsibility for it.

11. Do you ever want to do something just because God or your parents forbid it? Why?
Because we, like Eve, want total freedom with no limitations placed on us. Teens, in particular, crave this autonomy from parents.

12. Describe the situations in which it is easiest for you to yield to temptation.
with friends   at school   at home   at church
when angry at parents   haven't read Bible
while praying   when feeling independent

13. Which of the suggestions offered below could Eve have followed to withstand temptation?
She could have waited a few minutes, asked God about it, or run away.

14. In listening to Satan, Eve acted without thinking through the results of her actions.

15. List the pros and cons of the situation after Eve yielded to temptation:

Gained	Lost
Feeling of freedom	Innocence
More fruit to eat	Perfect relationship with God
Won a power struggle with God	Lost a power struggle with Satan

Wrap-up

Bring out a poster or large sheet of paper that says, "If in doubt, don't!"

Ask your teens how this statement applies to temptation. Allow for discussion. Ask them how delaying action can save us from yielding to temptation. Remind them of the choices Eve had (Question 13). Suggest that if she'd taken time to think, she might not have sinned.

Finish by giving them all a 3 x 5 card on which to copy, "If in doubt, don't!"

Prayer: Lord, help me to *want* to win over temptation and then help me to be stronger than it is.

LESSON 9

Guilt and Forgiveness

Lesson Goals
• to enlighten teens as to the nature and purpose of guilt.
• to offer helpful guidelines for handling guilt in our relationship with God.
• to encourage teens to apply these principles of handling guilt to their own lives.

Introduction

Guilt is a difficult issue at any age, but teens seldom know how to deal with it. Either their parents have guilt-tripped them into guilt as a way of life, or they don't even recognize guilt for what it is.

This lesson is designed to show guilt as a biblical concept, indeed even a help. Guilt, in the best sense, should act as a catalyst to lead us and offer this prayer of David's as a model for handling guilt in our lives.

Familiarize yourself with Psalm 51 as preparation for your own heart and for teaching.

Teacher Tips

You may want to begin this session by sharing instances of sin and guilt. However, your group may not be able to talk this freely among themselves. Either way, be sure to review briefly the sin of David with Bathsheba, which produced Psalm 51.

Ask for sharing on Question 2—how guilt feels. This is to be sure that guilt is recognized and the idea of a guilty conscience is understood.

Also emphasize the tendency of people to avoid God (Adam and Eve hiding in the garden of Eden). While this may be our tendency, we need not hide from God. He is always ready and willing to listen to us and forgive our sins. Emphasize how damaging it is to our relationship with God to avoid Him (perhaps you can illustrate this idea by using a relationship with another person as an example). Avoiding God leaves us with no comfort at all.

You may need to explain the concept of having a broken and contrite heart, so teens do not think in terms of broken hearts over a boyfriend or girlfriend. The biblical broken heart always relates to our closeness with God, which can be spoiled by our sin.

Read aloud the verses suggested in Question 11 to make sure your teens hear of God's willingness to forgive. (Note: you may need to explain that while God is always willing to forgive, that it does not mean that we can sin more often so He can forgive us repeatedly.

Pass out paper for teens to reply to Question 12 on how they usually handle guilty feelings.

Review Lesson 7 before beginning this lesson.

Answers

1. Check below what situations make you feel guilty.
• getting a friend in trouble
• lying/deception
• stealing/sneaking
• stealing someone's girlfriend/boyfriend
• not praying/reading the Bible
• talking behind someone's back
• acting greedily
• disobedience to parents
• anger at God

2. Describe how guilt feels.

3. Describe how you normally react or try to deal with guilt feelings.

4. Do you generally approach God or avoid Him when you feel guilty? Which do you think would be the most helpful?

5. Look through these verses to see how David felt. List below the feelings implied in these verses.
   2: sin feels dirty
   3: can't get hold of guilty feelings
   4: feels he has offended God
   5: feels like he's always been wrong
   8: bone-crushing sorrow
   9: wants to be rid of sin
   10: feels impure
   11: fear that God will leave him
   12: no joy; no spiritual strength
   14-5: can't praise God out of fear
   16: eager to please God, make amends

17: brokenhearted

On a scale of 1-10, rate David's feelings (1 = sad, 10 = great)

How does this compare to the last time you felt really guilty?
very similar   similar   different   no comparison

6. To see what David did about these guilty feelings, read through the verses given below and list the requests he made to God.
   1: Have mercy on me; blot out my transgressions
   2: Wash my iniquity; cleanse my sin
   7: Cleanse me; wash me
   8: Let me hear joy, gladness, rejoicing
   9: Blot out my iniquity
   10: Create a pure heart in me; renew a steadfast spirit in me
   11: Don't cast me away; don't take the Holy Spirit from me
   12: Restore my joy in salvation; help me remain true to you
   14: Save me from bloodguilt (the blood of Bathsheba's husband)
   15: Help me to praise you

7. Do you think David was right to approach God with these requests after he had blown it?
Knowing God's character helps us gather our courage to face Him after we've acted against His wishes.

8. Look for statements David made about God in the following verses. Write below how he described God.
   1: Unfailing love; great compassion
   4: God is a right and just judge
   6: God teaches truth and wisdom
   14: God is righteous
   16: God doesn't want offerings (after sinning)
   17: God desires a heart set to please him

9. What does David conclude God wants us to do after we've sinned?
God desires that we feel sorry for our sins.

10. Why does God want us to feel brokenhearted?
"Contrite and brokenhearted" here merely means that we feel truly sorry for the wrong we've done. If we are *truly* sorry, we are less likely to commit that same sin again. God wants to spare us those terrible guilt feelings of being alienated from Him.

We need to feel so sorry (brokenhearted) that we dislike the feelings after sinning and resolve not to sin again.

11. Psalm 51 doesn't tell us if God forgave David, but several other verses in the Bible tell us that God *does* forgive if we confess our sins and are truly sorry. Look up the following verses to see what God's forgiveness is like:

1 John 1:9
1 John 2:1, 2
Psalm 103:10-12
Matthew 18:21, 22

12. Think back to the last time you sinned and felt really guilty. List the steps you took in obtaining forgiveness (if you didn't, you may do it now).
God knows we are weak and sometimes do sinful things. But He is faithful to forgive us. Consider adopting the following principles as your "forgiveness plan."
   1. Think about why you did wrong (review the lesson on temptation).
   2. Admit that it was wrong. Sometimes we try to wriggle out of admitting our sins to ourselves or to God.
   3. Tell God what you did and why.
   4. Ask Him to forgive you.
   5. Remember His character; He is *willing* to forgive.
   6. Praise Him for forgiving you.

God knows we will fail. But no one has to hide from God. He doesn't stop loving us because we have sinned. But it *is* up to us to ask forgiveness. Why not ask His forgiveness today and free yourself from the "guilties"?

Wrap-up

To make sure a personal application is made, discuss the guidelines given at the end of the lesson.

Then give students paper and ask them to pray silently through these steps, applying them to the last sin(s) they can remember and asking God's forgiveness. Then close with a corporate prayer thanking God that He hears our confessions and forgives us.

Prayer: Dear God, I thank you that you forgive us again and again. In Jesus' name, Amen.

LESSON 10

Parents: A Love/Hate Relationship

Lesson Goal
• to transfer the idea of obedience to parents equals obedience to God and apply this idea to their home life and their relationship with parents.

Introduction

This topic could be a sticky one for some of your teens. Not all teens are fortunate (or unfortunate, in their minds) enough to have parents who try to teach them God's values. For these teens, the emphasis must be laid on obeying God.

Most of them will need help to think of their parents first as people, and then as guides preparing them for life with the Lord.

Even Christian teens with Christian parents will rebel to some degree against rules—just because they are desperate for independence. But at the same time, rules give them security (that is, something in life they can depend on). Though they may kick and scream, teens generally desire some system that orders life.

The bottom line to this concept is our need to learn to obey God. But this concept was explored explicitly in Lesson 9. There we learned that obedience to God makes life pleasant (besides being a way to worship God), whereas disobedience brings painful consequences. Disobedience to God equals sin. Obedience to parents equals obedience to God—until we are old enough to obey God of our own choosing.

Teacher Tips

1. Try to establish an open atmosphere so that students feel free to share problems in their relationships with their parents. You might set the stage by sharing your greatest difficulty with a parent when you were a teenager.

2. Don't get bogged down in anyone's specific problem (bedtime, laundry, etc.), but attempt to keep the discussion on rules, fairness, expectations, etc.

3. Help your teens to look at these situations from their parents' perspectives. Examples: What chores would you expect your 14-year-old son to do around the house? What time would you expect your 14-year-old daughter to be in on school nights if you were her mother?

4. List their greatest pet peeves on the chalkboard and take a poll to try to find general areas for discussion (rules, friends, sex).

5. Ask them to think in terms of compromise with their parents' rules. Discuss some examples.

6. Emphasize the aspect of obedience to God as the goal of parenting and of this lesson.

Answers

1. Choose your three most hated quirks of parental behavior.

2. Describe the ideal parent with ten adjectives (loving, funny, etc.)

3. Now, just for fun, describe what the ideal teenage son or daughter would be like.

4. Now, to see how everyone measures up, rate your family on a scale from 1-10 (10 = highest).
Mom
Dad
Me
My overall relationship with my parents

5. When you think of this relationship with your parents, did you ever wonder if God had any plans for parent/teen relationships? What verses can you think of that apply to this relationship?

6. Proverbs 17:6 says, "Parents are the pride of their children." In what aspect of your parents' lives could you take pride?
Mother   Father

7. Colossians 3:20 tells us: "Children, obey your parents in everything, for this pleases the Lord." Why do you think obeying your parents would please the Lord?

8. What reason is given for obedience in

21

Deuteronomy 6:2, 3?
 6:2—that you may enjoy long life
 6:3—that it may go well with you

9. What do you find significant in the thought that God is one?
There is only one God to obey. We are not to worship any other gods.

10. How does verse 5 tell us to love God? List one way you could love God with your
 heart/mind
 soul/feelings
 strength/actions

11. Verse 7 tells parents to impress these commandments on their children. Rewrite this verse in your own words.
A parent's job is to teach his or her children to obey him or her so that they learn to obey God when they are on their own.

12. Your parents may not write God's commands on your front gate, but try to think how they attempt to teach you to love and obey God by drawing a parallel to each of the ways mentioned in verses 7-9.
 Sit at home
 Walk along road
 Lie down
 Get up
 Symbols on hands/foreheads
 Symbols on doors/gates

13. What is your conclusion about a parent's job as seen in these verses? What does God expect parents to teach their children?
Parents are trying to teach their children obedience to Him.

14. If children are to learn to obey God (whom they can't see), they must first learn to obey their parents (whom they can see). Can you now think of your parents as trainers of obedience to God?

Write below three ways in which you have rebelled against your parents' rules. Looking at these three problem areas, what changes could you make in attempting to obey them?

Wrap-up

To offer teens another option besides just giving in to their parents' power (your teens' view), suggest a contract. Explain that sometimes parents and teens can profit from reaching an agreement on problem areas. This agreement would be worked out through discussion with parents on these areas of contention.

Example:

What I Expect	What Parents Expect

Curfew
Homework
Chores at Home
Church Attendance
Friends
Privacy
My Appearance
Social Behavior
Drugs, sex, drinking

After discussion, a contract can be drawn up listing agreements and punishments for breaking the agreement.

Close with a prayer for understanding and hearts eager to obey God.

Prayer: Dear God, help me to see that my parents are acting in love and for my benefit. Help me obey both them and You. In Jesus' name, amen.

LESSON 11

The Problem of Money

Lesson Goals
• to enable teens to define work as a pleasant and meaningful use of time.
• to get teens to separate the idea of work and money.
• to help teens focus on the importance of having other values in life besides obtaining money.

Introduction

This lesson will probably evoke strong feelings in your teens, because our society assumes money *is* the chief aim in life. Affluent American teenagers never even question this value, yet the Bible repeatedly warns against the corruption of money. Not only does it tempt people to dishonesty; it tempts them to spend their entire lives pursuing money rather than God. According to Genesis 2:15, God gave Adam all he needed for happiness: an ideal work situation and himself for a companion. This is a far cry from modern society's success-and-wealth syndrome.

Obtain a large jar of coins and place it in the center of the room for teens to ogle. Begin by asking who can think of a use for it. Allow several to suggest what they'd do with it.

Teacher Tips

During this discussion of money, try to steer talk away from how society is structured to how God intended. Teens need to hear how God meant for us to find satisfaction in life.

How we use money is *not* the focus of this lesson. The point to emphasize is this:
Money is not the chief aim in life.
Money is only an extra, secondary to finding satisfaction in life.

You might want to organize a debate around an extreme conclusion of society's thinking, such as found in one of the following statements:
 1. Money *is* the point of life.
 2. Money can buy anything you'll ever need.
 3. Work is something you endure to get your paycheck.

Allow three minutes' debate on one of these statements. Then, using the same teams, make them swap sides of the same argument. This promotes thinking through an issue from a different angle.

To facilitate general discussion:
 1. Allow no references to wealth or poverty to class members.
 2. Try to draw out the quieter teens to enrich discussion.
 3. Stress the value of meaning in life and its unrelatedness to money; that is, the value of things money can't buy—freedom, simple pleasures, nature, love, friendship.
 4. Try to avoid discussion of specific "things" and their desirability. Rather promote, thinking on the goodness of life, apart from material possessions.

Answers

1. If you were given $1000, what is the first thing you'd buy?
Second?
Absolute last thing you'd want to buy
Would you save any?

2. Plan a budget for an allowance of $50/month.
• tapes/records
• books
• toiletries/cosmetics
• movies/entertainment
• church
• impulse spending
• clothes
• savings

3. List below an example of wasteful use of money.

4. List a good cause to which you would give money

5. List one advantage and one disadvantage of a society that doesn't use money.
Advantages: There would be less corruption and dishonesty; less really poor or really rich.
Disadvantage: It would be harder to buy large items; some things would be harder to barter than others.

6. Name anything you can think of that is more important than money.
Time, freedom, satisfaction in work well done, people.

7. What was Adam's punishment for eating the fruit (v. 17)?
Adam's punishment is that now his work will not be enjoyable. It will become a struggle and a burden.

8. What does verse 18 say Adam will reap for his toil?
Thorns and thistles.

9. Describe Adam's work as depicted in verse 19.
Hard, never-ending, no satisfaction, just work until you die.

10. Do you find any mention of reward (money) for Adam's labor?
No.

11. What do you think was God's purpose for Adam originally (before he sinned and his efforts were cursed to fail?)
To enjoy his work and enjoy fellowship with God. Work was supposed to give purpose and fulfillment. One's reward was satisfaction with his work and having his needs supplied.

12. How does the idea of working "for the joy of it" fit into our society?
Most people in our society work strictly to earn money to find their satisfaction in buying things. Few people work just because they enjoy what they do.

Name the professions that you think people choose who are more interested in the work than in money.

13. If people really did find their reward in doing their work well, how would this change our society?
We'd see better quality workmanship; there would be less crime; society would be happier all around.

14. How does this idea change your attitude toward the desire for money?

15. How do you think our lives should be spent?
Enjoying our work as God intended.

16. Consider what is most important in your life.
- time or money
- hobby or money
- pleasure or money
- family or money
- nature or money
- friends or money
- education or money
- love or money
- freedom or money
- God's will or money

Wrap-up

Refer back to Question 16 and ask for volunteers to share what they consider most important in life. You might want to share what's more important than money in your life. Challenge them to reconsider how they plan to spend their lives. Suggest that there are better ways to spend your life than just pursuing money.

Prayer: Dear God, help me get the right perspective on money. Help me not to miss out on more important things in life by seeking money. In Jesus' name, amen.

LESSON 12

Fearing the Future

Lesson Goals
• to enable teens to grasp the concept that God is not limited in ideas or resources for salvaging the world's future.
• to help teens apply the concept of God's sovereignty to their individual life situations.

Introduction

This session may cause some teens to squirm inwardly. Their behavior may vary as they attempt to deal with uncomfortable issues such as anxiety over the future and thoughts of death. (Some will make jokes, some will argue, and some will go silent.)

Facing reality is healthier mentally than trying to pretend our fears don't exist. Teens need a safe place to deal with these topics openly and biblically.

They may also be feeling pressure to perform or succeed as they think about the future. They need to be reassured that God has a plan for the world and for them as individuals. Stress God's sovereignty as you guide today's discussion.

Teacher Tips

This lesson is not the time for pat answers or glossing over uncomfortable thoughts. During this discussion, do all you can to encourage free communication of *feelings,* not just ideas. Teens continually ooze feelings—half of which they can't understand. In discussing anxiety about the future, expressions of fear must not be mocked or smoothed over. If any group members are likely to insult others for expressing fears, you might want to make a statement to this effect before beginning.

In addition, teens need to hear adults' own fears or anxious thoughts, otherwise they assume adults have it all together. This makes teens feel even more anxious and inferior. But be sure to reaffirm your own belief that God is in control of you as well.

Answers

1. **What do you see yourself doing ten years from now?**
   • College?
   • Married?
   • Children? How many?
   • Job? What kind?
   • Dead?
   • Other

2. **When you think about the future, do you have an overall positive attitude or a negative one?**

3. **What scares you most about the future?**

4. **What events in the future are you eagerly awaiting?**

5. **How often do you think about nuclear war?**

6. **Do you think God could stop the world from being destroyed? How?**

   What do your friends say about the future?

7. **Look at Isaiah 40:26. What do you think God could do for you?**

8. **Look at Isaiah 40:11. What do you think are the "lambs" in this verse?**
   The lambs are us, His children, anyone who asks for His help.

   How does a shepherd care for His lambs? What do you think God could do for you?

9. **Read Isaiah 40:23. Does this verse help you to believe in God's control of the world, even though you can't see it?**

10. **List three "princes and rulers" (problems) you'd like God to "bring to naught" (solve) for you.**

11. **Read Isaiah 40:29-31. In what area of your life do you need strengthening so you can soar?**

12. **Read Isaiah 40:21, 22, 28, 29. What do these verses offer that you need?**

Potential answers: security of an everlasting kind, a source of strength, the wisdom of God, God's concern for individuals.

13. How has your thinking changed because of this lesson?

Potential answers: If God could create the world, He can do anything (v. 26); God has great power and strength (v. 26); God has a tender nature even though He is strong (v. 11); God rules the world even though we can't see Him ruling (v. 23); God cares enough for us to meet our needs (for strength; v. 29) God is everlasting.

14. List your conclusions from reading Isaiah 40.

15. What do you think the Bible promises for *your* future?

16. What can you begin to do *today* with this future?

17. What can you tell your friends who are afraid?

Wrap-up

Ask for volunteers to share insights from this lesson. One or two meaningful contributions is better than pulling information out of those who hesitate.

Then reaffirm your belief that God is in control of the future by sharing briefly a concern you have entrusted to God and have seen Him lovingly resolve.

Prayer: Dear God, if you could create the world and rule it, then you can take care of me. Help me to remember this when I am afraid. In Jesus' name, amen.

LESSON 13

Daily Time Alone With God (D.T.A.W.G.)

Lesson Goal
• to encourage teens to see the value of a D.T.A.W.G. and determine to make it a priority in their lives.

Introduction

Many teens have never considered the need for D.T.A.W.G. If this is the case, go slow in insisting on it. God wants us to come to Him willingly. He desires our worship, but He doesn't demand what we are not ready to give. Teens and adults alike need a living relationship with God before a quiet time can be seen as relevant or necessary.

Assuming your teens have encountered the reality of God, emphasize that time alone with God is the nourishment needed to keep this relationship alive.

Begin this session by asking teens to share times and places when God seemed very real to them. Then suggest that God is eager to meet with us any time and any place we desire.

Teaching Tips

The idea of daily prayer and Bible reading may not appeal to your teens. The aspect of meeting God in a personal way may be the best approach to arouse interest. Concentrate on God's desire to share intimately in our lives, the joy of friendship with God, and the benefits we derive from meeting with Him.

Also stress the individuality of this time. Suggest that they consider praying and praising in the way they find the most meaningful (singing, reading devotional literature geared to teens, taking nature walks, just being quiet).

Another much-needed emphasis is that of not feeling guilty when we miss a day (or days). Again, emphasize God's desire to meet with us and His grace, which allows for our weaknesses.

Share particularly helpful times with God from your own life to impress on them that God is real.

Answers

1. How do you spend your day? Estimate the amount of time you spend on the following activities in a day.

_____ sleeping	_____ school day
_____ eating	_____ sports
_____ television	_____ friends
_____ reading	_____ family, pet
_____ daydreaming	_____ talking on phone
_____ reading the Bible	_____ praying

2. From what source does most of your thinking come?

| _____ friends | _____ family |
| _____ television | _____ God |

3. Why do you think reading the Bible and prayer receive so little attention in our day's activities?
- too busy
- too boring
- don't understand it
- don't know how
- don't see any need for it

4. What effects might Bible reading and prayer have on your life?

5. According to King Darius, what is God able to do?
He can rescue and save; He can perform signs and wonders.

6. What two answers to Daniel's prayer do we see in these verses?
Daniel was saved from the lions; the king believed in God.

7. Why do you think Jesus would need to pray all night?
- lonely; wanted someone to talk to
- tired and bored
- didn't know God, His father, well enough
- got His strength from communicating with God

8. Describe the last time you felt weak, helpless, or in need of someone stronger to work out a problem for you.

9. List the six different words David used for biblical guidelines in Psalm 119:9-16.
word (vv. 9, 11, 16)
commands (10)
decrees (12, 16)
laws (13)
statutes (14)
precepts (15)

10. Now list what David does with God's Word
v. 9: living according to God's Word
v. 10: seek/not stray from God
v. 11: word hidden in his heart so he would not sin against God
v. 12: praise
v. 13: recount
v. 14: rejoice
v. 15: meditate/consider
v. 16: delight/not neglect

11. David truly seems to enjoy applying God's Word to his life. How can you do that? Read the following guidelines and fill in the blanks, adapting them to your life:

Time: Choose a time of day convenient for your D.T.A.W.G.

Place: Choose a place of privacy to meet regularly with God:

How to use this time:

1. Bible reading: I will read the book of _____ first (reading through the New Testament is a good way to begin).
2. Devotional books/studies: I will follow _____ for devotional reading.
3. Prayer: I will pray _____ minutes each day.
4. Prayer journal: I will pray for
- Family and friends
- Church needs
- World needs
- My own needs

Wrap-up

As a group, go over the last section on how to set up their own individual D.T.A.W.G. Discuss the best times and best places for privacy.

Then suggest possible resources for teen Bible studies, teen-oriented daily devotional books, etc. Draw on a chalkboard a mock prayer journal for them to concretize daily prayers. Brainstorm together for

27

prayer topics to help them recognize the broad scope for prayer.

Close by challenging your teens to include a D.T.A.W.G. in their lives. If appropriate for your group, break into pairs and pray for each other to persevere in a D.T.A.W.G.

Prayer: Dear God, help me to stay close to you always by meeting with You each day. In Jesus' name, amen.

LESSON 1

Who Am I?

Genesis 1

Do you enjoy walking outside on a clear evening? As you look at the stars, do they remind you how big our universe is? Does this cause you to think how small you are?

What other scenes/situations cause you to marvel at your smallness in the world?

- ❏ the ocean
- ❏ forests
- ❏ a thunderstorm
- ❏ a big city
- ❏ mountains
- ❏ a death

When you experience these things, you find yourself asking questions like, "Who am I? Where do I fit into the universe? How could I ever hope to know a God who must be bigger yet?"

The very first page of the Bible offers basic answers to these questions. Pretend that Genesis 1 (next page) was the only bit of the Bible you had ever seen. As you read, keep in mind these two questions: "What can I learn about myself?" and "What can I learn about God?"

1. The very first verse of the Bible describes God in terms of two basic facts. What are they?

a.

b.

This is important to me because:

29

> 1) In the beginning God created the heavens and the earth.
> 3) And God said, "Let there be light," and there was light.
> 6) And God said, "Let there be an expanse between the waters to separate water from water."
> 9) And God said, "Let the water under the sky be gathered to one place, and let dry ground appear." And it was so. . . . 11) Then God said, "Let the land produce vegetation: plants bearing seed according to their kinds and trees bearing fruit with seed in it, according to their various kinds." And it was so.
> 14) And God said, "Let there be lights in the expanse of the sky to separate the day from the night, and let them serve as signs to mark seasons and days and years . . ."
> 20) And God said, "Let the water teem with living creatures, and let birds fly above the earth across the expanse of the sky."
> 24) And God said, let the land produce living creatures according to their kinds: livestock, creatures that move along the ground, and wild animals, each according to its kind." And it was so. . . . 26) Then God said, "Let us make man in our image, in our likeness, and let them rule over the fish of the sea and the birds of the air, over the livestock, over all the earth, and over all the creatures that move along the ground."
> 31) God saw all that he had made, and it was very good. And there was evening, and there was morning—the sixth day.
> *Genesis 1:1, 3, 6, 9, 11, 14, 20, 24, 26, 31*

2. Genesis 1 does not give us any proof that God exists or explain how He began. What reasons can you think of why it does not do this?

3. What does your answer to Question 2 tell you about who you are and how you can know God? How long do you think people have been asking these questions?

4. What does Genesis 1 tell you about *how* God created our world?

5. If God could create out of nothing, what one trait must He possess?

6. Note the order in which God created. Briefly list God's "projects" during the first six days.

Day 1	Day 2	Day 3	Day 4	Day 5	Day 6

7. Could God have reversed that order? What seems right about the sequence God chose?

8. The way God planned His creation lets you see that, from the beginning, God was a _____ God. This is important to me because

9. God cared enough about the living things He created to give them the resources they needed. This gives you a hint of God's _____.

10. Does the thought of this huge God, as seen in Genesis 1, comfort you or frighten you? Why do you feel that way?

11. Based on what you've learned so far, do you think God is an "it" or a person?

31

12. What one thing does God do in verses 3, 6, 9, 11, 14, 20, 24, 26, 28, and 29? What does this tell you about what God can do with you?

13. What do the answers to questions 11 and 12 tell you about the possibility of your knowing God?

14. According to Genesis 1, what made men and women special compared to the rest of God's creation? In other words, what two special features did God plan for human beings (v. 1:26)?

15. If you were created in God's image, then what divine traits (ones you have already listed that relate to God) must *you* possess?

16. Does Genesis 1 tell you of anything else God created in His image? What does this tell you about yourself? About the possibility of knowing God?

I am _____ .

I can _____ .

Summary

    The characteristics of God seen in Genesis 1 are:
- ❑ existence
- ❑ ability to create
- ❑ power
- ❑ wisdom
- ❑ desire to communicate
- ❑ personhood
- ❑ has relationships

Check the two most important to you.

LESSON 2

Love Me, Love Me Not

Genesis 1:26, 27, Mark 3:13, 14

If you could instantly change three things about yourself, what would they be?

I would like to be

❑ taller
❑ smarter
❑ athletic
❑ outgoing
❑ popular
❑ older
❑ a leader
❑ thinner
❑ better-looking
❑ spiritual

Why did God make you as He did? Read Genesis 1:26, 27 to get a better understanding of how God made us.

> 26) Then God said, "Let us make man in our image, in our likeness, and let them rule over the fish of the sea and the birds of the air, over the livestock, over all the earth, and over all the creatures that move along the ground." 27) So God created man in his own image, in the image of God he created him; male and female he created them.
> *Genesis 1:26, 27*

1. From the beginning, God decided that people shouldn't all be exactly alike. What do you see in these verses to support that statement? Why didn't God make everyone the same?

2. As different as persons are, they all possess one common feature. What is it? Why is this common feature so important?

3. Thousands of years after God created men and women, He chose to come down to earth and become a person like them. What does this tell you of God's opinion of persons in general?

   ❑ He wasn't too smart
   ❑ He wanted to see what it would be like
   ❑ He liked people
   ❑ He came to help us

4. As Jesus was showing the world what God is like, He could have chosen several different methods. Jesus sometimes spoke to large crowds, but He spent most of His time with twelve men. How many of the disciples can you list by name? (If you have tried hard and are still stuck, Mark 3:16-19 will help.)

5. With the help of the appropriate Bible verses, link each disciple with the words best describing him.

   a. He sometimes seemed a little bit slow (John 6:5, 12:21, 14:8).

   b. He was probably a quiet sort, unless something aroused his temper (Mark 9:38, Luke 9:54, John 13:23, 20:21-24).
   c. He was a hard-nosed guy, perhaps with a scientific mind; he would believe only what he could see (John 11:16, 20:25).
   d. He still let his mom speak for him, even as an adult (Matthew 20:20, 21).
   e. He betrayed Jesus (Matthew 26:47-49).

   f. He was a good leader, but sometimes put his foot in his mouth (Matthew 16:16, 22).
   g. He was a political activist (Acts 1:13).

   h. He was quick to decide, sometimes a good trait and sometimes not. Be careful; this one seems to have two names (John 1:46-49).
   i. He was unknown; the Bible tells us nothing but his father's name (Acts 1:13).

j. He must have been a quiet man; all we know is that he asked one question (another one with two names) (John 14:22).
k. He lived in the shadow of his brother, yet did well at bringing people to Jesus (John 1:40, 6:8).
l. He had not been the most respectable guy before he met Jesus (Matthew 9:9, 11).

6. For each of the following sentences, circle the word that is true.

    a. The disciples were all quite (similar / different).
    b. The disciples (did / did not) always follow Jesus well.
    c. The Bible (does / does not) tell a lot about each disciple.

7. Why did Jesus choose disciples who were so different from each other and from Him?

8. Based on your answers to the last two questions, what do you think about each of the following statements?

    a. Jesus loves one type of person (maybe the smart or the beautiful) more than the rest.

    b. Jesus chooses only those who do everything right to be His followers.

    c. Those who stand out in the crowd are more important to God than "ordinary" people.

---

13) Jesus went up into the hills and called to him those he wanted, and they came to him. 14) He appointed twelve—designating them apostles—that they might be with him and that he might send them out to preach.
Mark 3:13, 14

9. These verses show us Jesus as He was choosing the twelve disciples. What do they tell us about how He felt toward them?

What can you learn about how Jesus feels about you?

All too often, when you are feeling down about yourself, it's because you are comparing yourself to someone else whom you think is better than you. Even Jesus' disciples fell into this habit (see Mark 9:33, 34 and Luke 22:24).

10. Verse 13 says Jesus called to himself "those whom He wanted." Why do you think Jesus wants *you* to be with Him?

11. Check below those statements that enable you to better accept yourself *just as you are right now:*

    ❏ God made me who I am
    ❏ God made me for a purpose
    ❏ Jesus wants me to be with Him
    ❏ I am special because I am uniquely made
    ❏ I don't have to be like anyone else
    ❏ God accepts me just as I am, with all my "warts"
    ❏ I don't have to be perfect to be loved

12. How is your thinking about yourself changed by the knowledge that God accepts you?

LESSON 3

Free to Be Me

Genesis 1:28-30, 2:15-18

What would you do if you pulled up to a traffic signal on which both the red and green were lit? Have you ever felt that people around you gave opposite signals to you? On one hand, you hear, "Be yourself! Develop your own unique personality." On the other hand, "Be like everyone else. Do what we say! Conform!"

Deciding between these voices can be difficult. You want to be faithful to yourself, but life seems easier when you give in to the wishes of others. Which is better, to be yourself, or to be what others want?

List some choices you make daily.

Let's see how God's plan gave Adam and Eve power over the world.

> 28) God blessed them and said to them, "Be fruitful and increase in number; fill the earth and subdue it. Rule over the fish of the sea and the birds of the air and over every living creature that moves on the ground."
>
> 29) Then God said, "I give you seed-bearing plant on the face of the earth and every tree that has fruit with seed in it. They will be yours for food. 30) And to all the beasts of the earth and all the birds of the air and all the creatures that move on the ground—everything that has the breath of life in it—I give every green plant for food." And it was so.
>
> ....
>
> 2:15) The Lord God took the man and put him in the Garden of Eden to work it and take care of it. 16) And the Lord God commanded the man, "You are free to eat from any tree in the garden; 17) but you must not eat from the tree of the knowledge of good and evil, for when you eat of it you will surely die."
>
> 18) Then the Lord God said, "It is not good for the man to be alone. I will make a helper suitable for him."
>
> *Genesis 1:28-30, 2:15-18*

1. How does this gift of power reflect God's image in Adam and Eve?

2. What limits did God place on Adam and Eve's power?

3. Within these limits, did Adam and Eve still possess great freedom? What types of choices remained open to them? Adam and Eve could:

   - ❏ eat strawberries all day
   - ❏ make love
   - ❏ compose songs
   - ❏ sleep all day
   - ❏ get acquainted
   - ❏ argue over names for animals
   - ❏ breed pedigreed cats
   - ❏ organize the SPCA

Let's look at another Old Testament character and his choices. Listen as your teacher summarizes the Old Testament story of Joseph, as found in Genesis 37 and 39.

On several occasions, Joseph decided not to do what other people wanted. Listed below are four incidents from his early life. Examine each of these in terms of Questions 4-7.

	His dreams (Genesis 37:3-11)	Sold into slavery (Genesis 37:25-28, 39:1-4)	Potiphar's wife (Genesis 39:5-19)	Unjust prison term (Genesis 39:19-23)
4. What did the people around Joseph hope (or expect) he would do?				
5. What did Joseph choose to do?				
6. What happened as a result?				
7. Do you feel Joseph made the best decision? Why?				

8. In each of the four situations, Joseph chose not to conform to what others expected of him. Is this always the best decision? Why?

9. What guidelines can you adopt to help you make decisions?

   Before I decide, I can _____.

   To help me weigh the options, I should _____.

   If I have doubts, I _____.

   To keep me from messing up, I should _____.

10. List three steps in the decision-making process.

   1. _____.

   2. _____.

   3. _____.

11. Apply these three steps to a decision you are considering right now in your life.

   1. _____.

   2. _____.

   3. _____.

LESSON 4

Why Should I Care About My Neighbors?

Genesis 4:8, 9; Luke 10:30-36

1. List your three major concerns in life (in priority order).

2. Where did the needs of others figure into your concerns?
   - ❏ high on the list
   - ❏ just made the list
   - ❏ not at all

Why should others be my concern? Let's look at two passages of Scripture to answer this question.

---

8) Now Cain said to his brother Abel, "Let's go out to the field." And while they were in the field, Cain attacked his brother Abel and killed him.
9) Then the Lord said to Cain, "Where is your brother Abel?"
"I don't know," he replied. "Am I my brother's keeper?"

Genesis 4: 8, 9

---

3. Was Cain concerned for his brother's welfare?   Yes   No
   Should he have been?   Yes   No

4. What do you think it means to be "your brother's keeper" (or sister's).
   - ❏ feeding/clothing them
   - ❏ babysitting/odd jobs for friends
   - ❏ helping the poor and homeless
   - ❏ loving people as they are
   - ❏ all of the above

Being your brother's (or sister's) keeper might mean anything! It involves caring enough about them to put their needs above your own. Let's look at an example of someone who did this beautifully.

> 30) In reply Jesus said, "A man was going down from Jerusalem to Jericho, when he fell into the hands of robbers. They stripped him of his clothes, beat him and went away, leaving him half dead. 31) A priest happened to be going down the same road, and when he saw the man, he passed by on the other side. 32) So too, a Levite, when he came to the place and saw him, passed by on the other side. 33) But a Samaritan, as he traveled, came where the man was, and when he saw him, he took pity on him. 34) He went to him and bandaged his wounds, pouring on oil and wine. Then he put the man on his own donkey, took him to an inn and took care of him. 35) The next day he took out two silver coins and gave them to the innkeeper. 'Look after him,' he said, 'and when I return, I will reimburse you for any extra expense you may have.'
>
> 36) "Which of these three do you think was a neighbor to the man who fell into the hands of robbers?"
>
> *Luke 10:30-36*

5. List the events that happened to the victim in this story.

   a. _____

   b. _____

   c. _____

   d. _____

6. Now imagine that you are the first person to walk by this man. You see the blood and you hear him moan. Write below what your first reaction to this situation would be.

7. Now look at verse 33 to see what the Samaritan did for the victim. List his actions below:

   a. _____

   b. _____

   c. _____

   d. _____

   e. _____

   f. _____

8. Why do you think the Samaritan went to all this bother for a stranger?

9. Verse 29 says that Jesus told this story to answer the question, "Who is my neighbor?" How do you think the victim was the Samaritan's "neighbor?"

10. In verse 27 Jesus says we are to love God with all our hearts and love our neighbors as ourselves. Define what it would mean in your life to love one of your "neighbors" as you love yourself.

11. Who are your neighbors?

12. Who among your neighbors (in the broadest sense) is in need of help?

13. Check the types of help they need on this list:

   ❑ food
   ❑ clothing
   ❑ friendship
   ❑ babysitting/odd jobs
   ❑ invitation to your house
   ❑ someone to stand up for them
   ❑ other

   ❑ money
   ❑ prayer
   ❑ someone to listen
   ❑ help with schoolwork
   ❑ invitation to church

14. Which of these can you provide for one of your "neighbors" in need?

LESSON 5

Life Is a-Changin'

Isaiah 40

1. How often do you change your:
   - ❑ hairstyle
   - ❑ best friend
   - ❑ weight
   - ❑ favorite TV show
   - ❑ church
   - ❑ favorite teacher
   - ❑ posters on your wall
   - ❑ girlfriend or boyfriend
   - ❑ bedtime
   - ❑ style of dress
   - ❑ favorite sport
   - ❑ makeup
   - ❑ ideas of right and wrong

2. List five things in your life that you never intend to change.

3. What aspects of your life would you most like to change?

4. What one thing (or person) in your life do you consider the most dependable?

5. Do you ever feel that life changes too fast?

   Often   Sometimes   Never

6. Do you think God ever changes?

   Yes   No   Not sure

Let's see what Isaiah 40 has to say about change:

45

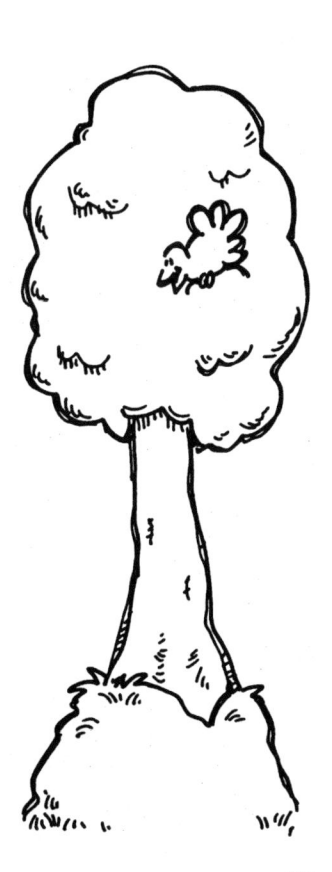

> 6) A voice says, "Cry out."
>   And I said, "What shall I cry?"
> "All men are like grass,
>   and all their glory is like the flowers of the field.
> 7) The grass withers and the flowers fall,
>   because the breath of the Lord blows on them.
>   Surely the people are grass.
> 8) The grass withers and the flowers fall,
>   but the word of our God stands forever."
> *Isaiah 40:6-8*

7. Look at the contrast in these verses and complete the following thoughts to make them true (according to verses 6-8).

   Humanity (will / will not) last forever.

   God's Word (will / will not) last forever.

Now we see God and His Word last forever. Let's look at His attitude toward us. Read Isaiah 40:10-14.

> 10) See, the Sovereign Lord comes with power,
>   and his arm rules for him.
> See, his reward is with him,
>   and his recompense accompanies him.
> 11) He tends his flock like a shepherd:
>   He gathers the lambs in his arms
> and carries them close to his heart;
>   He gently leads those that have young.
> 12) Who has measured the waters in the hollow of his hand,
>   or with the breadth of his hand marked off the heavens?
> Who has held the dust of the earth in a basket,
>   or weighed the mountains on the scales
>   and the hills in a balance?
> 13) Who has understood the Spirit of the Lord,
>   or instructed him as his counselor?
> 14) Whom did the Lord consult to enlighten him,
>   and who taught him the right way?
> Who was it that taught him knowledge
>   or showed him the path of understanding?
> *Isaiah 40:10-14*

8. What adjective in this list best describes God as found in verse 10?•
   - ❑ helpless
   - ❑ unconcerned
   - ❑ powerful
   - ❑ interested

9. What do the sheep (flock) represent in verse 11?

   How does it make you feel to think of God carrying you in His arms?
   - ❑ afraid
   - ❑ unconcerned
   - ❑ silly
   - ❑ safe

10. What impression do verses 12, 13 give you of God?

Verses 6-8 tell us God doesn't change. Then verses 10-14 tell us He does care for us. Let's see what else we can find out about God in verses 21-31 that relates to our lives.

> 21) Do you not know?
>   Have you not heard?
> Has it not been told you from the beginning?
>   Have you not understood since the earth was founded?
> 22) He sits enthroned above the circle of the earth,
>   and its people are like grasshoppers.
> He stretches out the heavens like a canopy,
>   and spreads then out like a tent to live in.
> 23) He brings princes to naught
>   and reduces the rulers of this world to nothing.
> 24) No sooner are they planted,
>   no sooner are they sown,
>   no sooner do they take root in the ground,
> than he blows on them and they wither,
>   and a whirlwind sweeps them away like chaff. . . .
> 28) Do you not know?
>   Have you not heard?
> The Lord is the everlasting God,
>   the Creator of the ends of the earth.
> He will not grow tired or weary,
>   and his understanding no one can fathom.
> 29) He gives strength to the weary
>   and increases the power of the weak.

> 30) Even youths grow tired and weary,
>   and young men stumble and fall;
> 31) but those who hope in the Lord
>   will renew their strength.
> They will soar on wings like eagles;
>   they will run and not grow weary,
>   they will walk and not be faint.
>   *Isaiah 40:21-24, 28-31*

11. List the amazing things God can do from the following verses:

    22

    23

    24

    28

    28

    29

12. What impression do these verses give you of God?

13. Now list the ways He can help *you*.

    v. 29 (2)

    v. 31 (4)

14. Through all the change and uncertainty in your life, you have a powerful, unchanging God to help you. Write below one way God can help you face the uncertainty that most scares you. God can give you strength to "soar" over the problem of:

LESSON 6

What's With Sex Anyway?

Genesis 2:20-25; 2 Samuel 11

Circle True or False according to your beliefs concerning sex:

God created sex, so He knows best how it should be used	T	F
Sex is OK between two people who love each other, married or not	T	F
God is mean to restrict intercourse to marriage	T	F
Sex is God's gift, so we can use it any way we choose	T	F
Sex is strictly a physical act, with no life-changing effects	T	F
I must look and act sexy if I don't want to be left out	T	F
To husbands and wives, sex is a beautiful means of communication	T	F
Sex is necessary to hold on to a boyfriend or girlfriend	T	F
The church is out of touch to forbid sex outside of marriage	T	F
Sex includes mind, body, and emotions; it is most meaningful in a lasting relationship	T	F
Decisions about sex should be left to each individual	T	F
The Bible presents sex as good, and best if kept for marriage	T	F

If these questions leave you somewhat confused about whose ideas on sex are correct, look at Genesis 2:20-25.

> 20) So the man gave names to all the livestock, the birds of the air and all the beasts of the field.
> But for Adam no suitable helper was found. 21) So the Lord God caused the man to fall into a deep sleep; and while he was sleeping, he took one of the man's ribs and closed up the place with flesh. 22) Then the Lord God made a woman from the rib he had taken out of the man, and he brought her to the man.
> The man said, "This is now bone of my bones and flesh of my flesh; she shall be called 'woman,' for she was taken out of man." 24) For this reason a man will leave his father and mother and be united to his wife, and they will become one flesh.
> The man and his wife were both naked, and they felt no shame.
> *Genesis 2:20-25*

These verses imply that Adam wasn't happy even in this perfect environment. What emotion do you think Adam was experiencing?

1. What sort of role was Eve created to fulfill in Adam's life?

2. Verse 22 says God made Eve by taking out one of Adam's ribs. What sort of relationship did God intend Adam and Eve to have?

3. When Adam exclaimed about Eve, "Bone of my bone and flesh of my flesh!" (v. 23) what emotion do you think Adam felt toward Eve?
   - ❏ anger
   - ❏ lust
   - ❏ joy
   - ❏ pain
   - ❏ frustration
   - ❏ excitement
   - ❏ love
   - ❏ other

4. Verse 24 says that man and woman will leave their parents to live together. What kind of relationship does this imply? What does the word "cleave" mean?

5. Why do you think verse 26 was included in the Bible?

6. God obviously intended sex to be a part of male/female relationships, but why do you suppose He restricted it to marriage?

Let's look at what results from taking sex anywhere you please. Notice what happened to David when he seduced Bathsheba.

2) One evening David got up from his bed and walked around on the roof of his palace. From the roof he saw a woman bathing. The woman was very beautiful, 3) and David sent someone to find out about her. The man said, "Isn't this Bathsheba, the daughter of Eliam and the wife of Uriah the Hittite?" 4) Then David sent messengers to get her. She came to him, and he slept with her. (She had purified herself from her uncleanness.) Then she went back home. 5) The woman conceived and sent word to David, saying, "I am pregnant." . . .

14) In the morning David wrote a letter to Joab and sent it with Uriah. 15) In it he wrote, "Put Uriah in the front line where the fighting is fiercest. Then withdraw from him so he will be struck down and die. . . ."

26) When Uriah's wife heard that her husband was dead, she mourned for him. 27) After the time of mourning was over, David had her brought to his house, and she became his wife and bore him a son. But the thing David had done displeased the Lord.

2 Samuel 11:2-5, 14, 15, 26, 27

7. What was wrong with David watching a beautiful woman taking a bath?

8. What could Bathsheba have done to avoid exciting David?

9. Put the events of the story in the proper order.

　　___ a. Bathsheba gets pregnant
　　___ b. Bathsheba bathes on rooftop at night
　　___ c. David sends for Bathsheba
　　___ d. David sees Bathsheba bathing
　　___ e. Bathsheba comes to David
　　___ f. David lusts for Bathsheba
　　___ g. David seduces Bathsheba

10. Write below what David and Bathsheba could have done next.

What did David, king of Israel, choose to do?

11. Verse 17 tells us that Uriah, Bathsheba's husband, did die in battle. How do you think David and Bathsheba felt?
    - ❏ glad
    - ❏ relieved
    - ❏ guilty
    - ❏ unconcerned
    - ❏ sorry
    - ❏ other

12. After that, Bathsheba mourned Uriah (it was custom), moved into David's house, and had a baby boy. What word describes the Lord's reaction to this?

13. The Lord was so displeased that He caused the baby to become ill and die (12:15-18). Look at David's reaction in verse 16. List what David did.

14. Do you think David thought seducing Bathsheba worth killing her husband and their baby?

15. What conclusions do you draw from this story about the results of misusing sex?

16. Could it be that God *knows* that misusing sex causes pain for us? List below three ways misusing sex can cause misery for you.

LESSON 7

Evil in the World

Genesis 3

1. Which of the following acts do you think best depicts evil?
   - ❏ abortion
   - ❏ war
   - ❏ starving nations
   - ❏ murder/crime
   - ❏ selfishness
   - ❏ hating God
   - ❏ disease

2. On a scale of 1 to 10 (10 = highest), rate these results of evil as they affect *your* life. How much do you suffer because of _____?

abortion	1 2 3 4 5 6 7 8 9 10
war	1 2 3 4 5 6 7 8 9 10
starving nations	1 2 3 4 5 6 7 8 9 10
murder/crime	1 2 3 4 5 6 7 8 9 10
selfishness	1 2 3 4 5 6 7 8 9 10
hating God	1 2 3 4 5 6 7 8 9 10
disease	1 2 3 4 5 6 7 8 9 10

3. Compare Genesis 1:31 and 2:25 with 3:7, 8 and 3:23, 24.

   1:31 and 2:25   3:7, 8 and 3:23, 24

4. Write below why you think there is evil in the world.

> 1:31) God saw all that he had made, and it was very good. And there was evening, and there was morning—the sixth day. . . . 2:25) The man and his wife were both naked, and they felt no shame.
>
> 3:7) Then the eyes of both of them were opened, and they realized they were naked; so they sewed fig leaves together and made coverings for themselves. 8) Then the man and his wife heard the sound of the Lord God as he was walking in the garden in the cool of the day, and they hid from the Lord God among the trees of the garden. . . . 23) So the Lord God banished him from the Garden of Eden to work the ground from which he had been taken. 24) After he drove the man out, he placed on the east side of the Garden of Eden cherubim and a flaming sword flashing back and forth to guard the way to the tree of life.
>
> *Genesis 1:31; 2:25; 3:7, 8, 23, 24*

5. Refer to Genesis 3:1-7 (p. 57) and analyze as follows:

Person	What he(she) did	What happened then	What choice was involved

6. Who was evil in the passage?

7. What was evil in the passage?
   ❏ talking to the serpent
   ❏ eating the fruit
   ❏ doing what the serpent wanted
   ❏ doing what God had forbidden
   ❏ the serpent doubting God's command

8. What two words describe the serpent (v. 1)?

9. Define what the serpent *really* meant by the following statements:

   "Did God say, 'You shall not eat of any tree in the garden?'"

   He really meant:

   "You will not die."

   He really meant:

10. What then was evil in the serpent? What other name does the Bible use for the serpent?

11. How does evil affect your life? Answer the following true or false.
    - ❑ I get really concerned about starving people.
    - ❑ If I saw a parent abusing a child, I'd try to stop him.
    - ❑ Evil in the world really doesn't touch my life.
    - ❑ I would participate in a peace march near my home.
    - ❑ I don't really get upset when I read the newspapers.
    - ❑ I believe disease is due to evil in the world.

12. Do you think God meant for the world to be full of evil? Why do you think He allowed the serpent to defile His world?
    - ❑ He was trying an experiment.
    - ❑ He couldn't stop the serpent.
    - ❑ He gave Eve a choice whom to love and serve.
    - ❑ He knew Eve would sin eventually.

God planned the world to be good. But He gave us the freedom to choose right or wrong for ourselves. Eve chose her own way over God's. We all pay a high price when we choose our own way over God's.

13. List below two or three ways in which you have been choosing your own way over what you know to be God's desires.

    Your way   God's command

14. Write below, in two or three sentences, how you'd like to live your Christian life.

56

LESSON 8

Temptation

Genesis 3

List below three things you really want and how to go about getting them.

I really want	How I can get this for myself	
	Honestly (God's way)	Dishonestly (Satan's way)
1.		
2.		
3.		

> 1) Now the serpent was more crafty than any of the wild animals the Lord God had made. He said to the woman, "Did God really say, 'You must not eat from any tree in the garden?'"
> 2) The woman said to the serpent, "We may eat fruit from the trees in the garden, 3) but God did say, 'You must not eat fruit from the tree that is in the middle of the garden, and you must not touch it, or you will die.'"
> 4) "You will not surely die," the serpent said to the woman. 5) "For God knows that when you eat of it your eyes will be opened, and you will be like God, knowing good and evil."
> 6) When the woman saw that the fruit of the tree was good for food and pleasing to the eye, and also desirable for gaining wisdom, she took some and ate it. She also gave some to her husband, who was with her, and he ate it. 7) Then the eyes of both of them were opened, and they realized they were naked; so they sewed fig leaves together and made coverings for themselves.
>
> *Genesis 3:1-7*

The real question: How do I win over the temptation of dishonest shortcuts to get what I want?

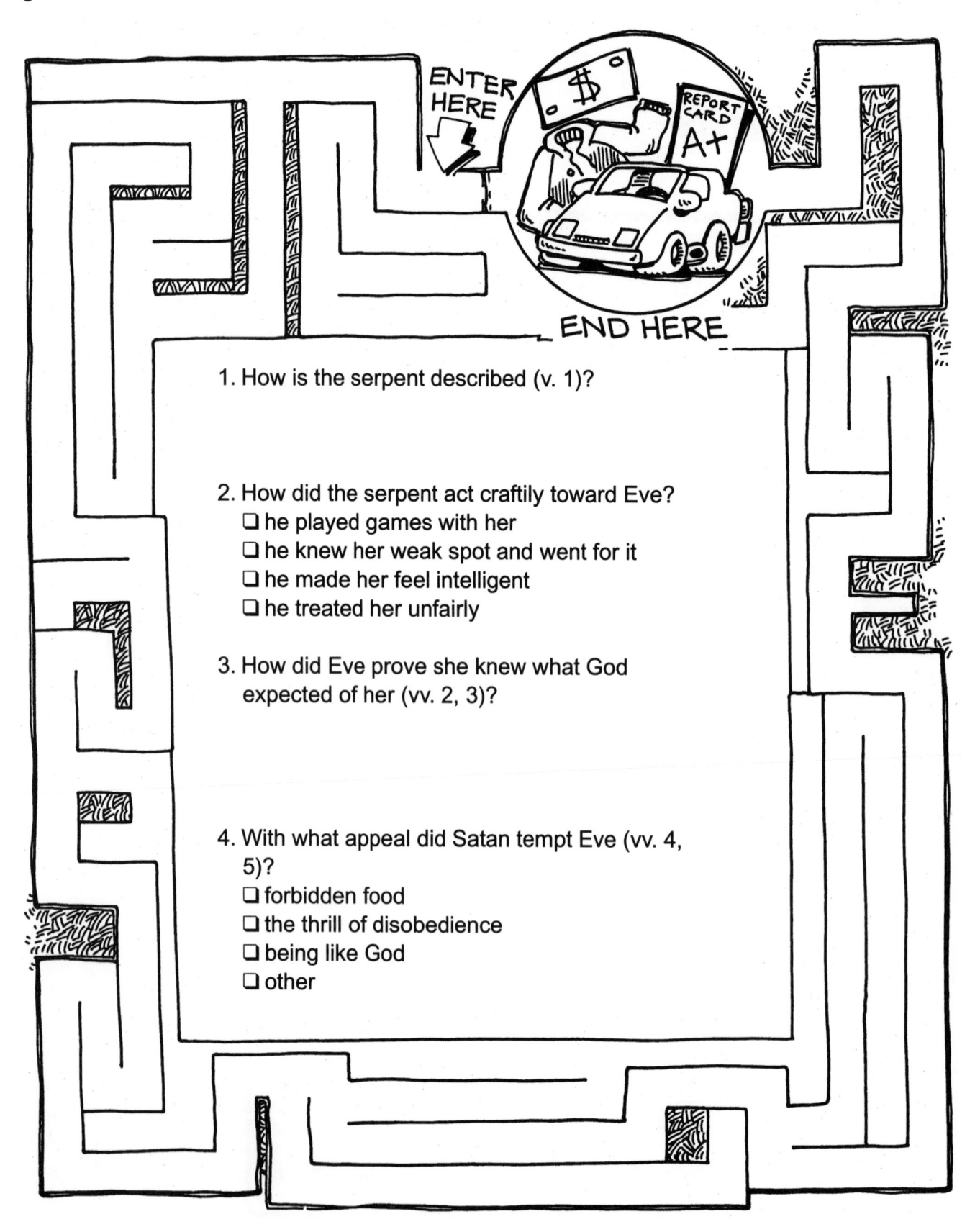

1. How is the serpent described (v. 1)?

2. How did the serpent act craftily toward Eve?
   ❏ he played games with her
   ❏ he knew her weak spot and went for it
   ❏ he made her feel intelligent
   ❏ he treated her unfairly

3. How did Eve prove she knew what God expected of her (vv. 2, 3)?

4. With what appeal did Satan tempt Eve (vv. 4, 5)?
   ❏ forbidden food
   ❏ the thrill of disobedience
   ❏ being like God
   ❏ other

5. What were Eve's choices for response in this situation?

6. Why do you think God allowed Eve a choice (temptation)?

7. What three things helped Eve give in to temptation (v. 6)?

8. Describe an ad or commercial you've seen that is based on food appeal, eye appeal, or promises that you'll be thought intelligent, sexy, or "with it." Did it sell you on their product?

   Did these ads use Christian or nonChristian principles to sell their product?

9. What two things did Eve stand to lose by eating the fruit?

10. Why do you think Eve couldn't be satisfied with some fruit from another tree that was allowed?

11. Do you ever want to do something just because God or your parents forbid it? Why do you think that is?

12. Describe the situations in which it is easiest for you to yield to temptation.

   Where?
   ❏ with friends
   ❏ at school
   ❏ at home
   ❏ at church

   When?
   ❏ when angry at parents
   ❏ haven't read Bible
   ❏ while praying
   ❏ when feeling independent

13. Which of the suggestions offered below could Eve have followed to withstand temptation?
   ❏ waited a few minutes
   ❏ argued with Satan
   ❏ discussed it with Adam
   ❏ prayed/asked God about it
   ❏ run away
   ❏ offered Satan some fruit too
   ❏ not listened to Satan's arguments

14. In listening to Satan, Eve

15. List the pros and cons of the situation after Eve yielded to temptation:

   Gained   Lost

Remember, temptation is not a sin. Temptation is a choice. Sin is knowing right and deliberately choosing wrong In what areas are you tempted to choose wrongly?

What can you do to help yourself resist temptation? (Refer back to Question 12.)

LESSON 9

Guilt and Forgiveness

Psalm 51

1. Check below what situations make you feel guilty.
   - ❑ getting a friend in trouble
   - ❑ lying/deception
   - ❑ stealing/sneaking
   - ❑ stealing someone's girlfriend/boyfriend
   - ❑ not praying/reading the Bible
   - ❑ talking behind someone's back
   - ❑ acting greedily
   - ❑ disobedience to parents
   - ❑ anger at God

2. Describe how guilt feels.

3. Describe how you normally react or try to deal with guilt feelings.

4. Do you generally approach God or avoid Him when you feel guilty?

   Which do you think would be the most helpful?

5. After David had his affair with Bathsheba, he felt guilty. He wasn't sure God could ever forgive him. Psalm 51 is the prayer David wrote to approach God with his guilty feelings and ask forgiveness. Look through the verses on the next page to see how David felt. List in the margin the feelings implied in these verses.

1) Have mercy on me, O God,
   according to your unfailing love;
   according to your great compassion
   blot out my transgressions.
2) Wash away all my iniquity
   and cleanse me from my sin.
3) For I know my transgressions,
   and my sin is always before me.
4) Against you, you only, have I sinned
   and done what is evil in your sight,
   so that you are proved right when you speak
   and justified when you judge.
5) Surely I have been a sinner from birth,
   sinful from the time my mother conceived me.
6) Surely you desire truth in the inner parts;
   you teach me wisdom in the inmost place.
7) Cleanse me with hyssop, and I will be clean;
   wash me, and I will be whiter than snow.
8) Let me hear joy and gladness;
   let the bones you have crushed rejoice.
9) Hide your face from my sins
   and blot out all my iniquity.
10) Create in me a pure heart, O God,
    and renew a steadfast spirit within me.
11) Do not cast me from your presence
    or take your Holy Spirit from me.
12) Restore to me the joy of your salvation
    and grant me a willing spirit, to sustain me.
13) Then I will teach transgressors your ways,
    and sinners will turn back to you.
14) Save me from bloodguilt, O God,
    the God who saves me,
    and my tongue will sing of your righteousness.
15) O Lord, open my lips,
    and my mouth will declare your praise.
16) You do not delight in sacrifice, or I would bring it;
    you do not take pleasure in burnt offerings.
17) The sacrifices of God are a broken spirit;
    a broken and contrite heart,
    O God, you will not despise.

Psalm 51:1-17

On a scale of 1-10, rate David's feelings (1 = sad, 10 = great)

1 2 3 4 5 6 7 8 9 10

How does this compare to the last time you felt really guilty?
very similar   similar   different   no comparison

6. To see what David did about these guilty feelings, read through the verses given below and list the requests he made to God. (Note: some verses make more than one request.)

    1 (2)

    2 (2)

    7 (2)

    8 (3)

    9
    10
    11 (2)

    12 (2)

    14

    15

7. Do you think David was right to approach God with these requests after he had blown it?

8. Knowing God's character helps us gather courage to face Him after we've acted against His wishes. Look for statements David made about God in these verses. Write below how he described God.

    1

    4

    6

    14

    16

    17

9. What does David conclude God wants us to do after we've sinned?

10. Why does God want us to feel brokenhearted?

11. Psalm 51 doesn't tell us if God forgave David, but several other verses in the Bible tell us that God *does* forgive if we confess our sins and are truly sorry. Look up the following verses to see what God's forgiveness is like:
    1 John 1:9
    1 John 2:1, 2
    Psalm 103:10-12
    Matthew 18:21, 22

12. Think back to the last time you sinned and felt really guilty. List the steps you took in obtaining forgiveness.

1.

2.

3.

4.

5.

(If you didn't, you may do it now.)

Forgiveness Plan

God knows we sin, but He is faithful to forgive us. Consider adopting the following principles as your "forgiveness plan."

1. Think about why you did wrong (review lesson on temptation).
2. Admit that it was wrong. Sometimes we try to wriggle out of admitting our sins to ourselves or to God.
3. Tell God what you did and why.
4. Ask Him to forgive you.
5. Remember His character; He is *willing* to forgive.
6. Praise Him for forgiving you.

LESSON 10

Parents: A Love/Hate Relationship

Deuteronomy 6:1-9

1. Choose your three most hated quirks of parental behavior.
   - ❑ nagging
   - ❑ disliking your friends
   - ❑ complaints about your appearance
   - ❑ making you go to church
   - ❑ expecting good grades
   - ❑ forbidding sex (or drinking)
   - ❑ double standards
   - ❑ telling you what to think
   - ❑ snooping in your things
   - ❑ demanding work around the house

2. Describe the ideal parent with ten adjectives (loving, funny, etc.)

1. _____ 2. _____ 3. _____

4. _____ 5. _____ 6. _____

7. _____ 8. _____

9. _____ 10. _____

65

3. Now, just for fun, describe what the ideal teenage son or daughter would be like.

4. Rate your family on a scale from 1-10.

   Mom   1   2   3   4   5   6   7   8   9   10
   Dad   1   2   3   4   5   6   7   8   9   10
   Me   1   2   3   4   5   6   7   8   9   10

   My overall relationship with my parents:

   1   2   3   4   5   6   7   8   9   10

5. When you think of this relationship with your parents, did you ever wonder if God had any plans for parent/teen relationships? What verses can you think of that apply to this relationship?

6. Proverbs 17:6 says, "Parents are the pride of their children." In what aspects of your parents' lives could you take pride?

   Mother   Father

7. Colossians 3:20 tells us: "Children, obey your parents in everything, for this pleases the Lord." Why do you think obeying your parents would please the Lord?

Let's look at an old concept: obedience to God and your parents.

> 1) These are the commands, decrees and laws the Lord your God directed me to teach you to observe in the land that you are crossing the Jordan to possess, 2) so that you, your children and their children after them may fear the Lord your God as long as you live by keeping all his decrees and commands that I give you, and that you may enjoy long life. 3) Hear, O Israel, and be careful to obey so that it may go well with you and that you may increase greatly in a land flowing with milk and honey, just as the Lord, the God of your fathers, promised you.
>
> 4) Hear, O Israel: The Lord our God, the Lord is one. 5) Love the Lord your God with all your heart and with all your soul and with all your strength. 6) These commandments that I give you today are to be upon your hearts. 7) Impress them on your children. Talk about them when you sit at home and when you walk along the road, when you lie down and when you get up. 8) Tie them as symbols on your hands and bind them on your foreheads. 9) Write them on the doorframes of your houses and on your gates.
>
> *Deuteronomy 6:1-9*

8. What reasons are given for obedience in verses 6:2 and 6:3?

9. What do you find significant in the thought that God is one?

10. How does verse 5 tell us to love God? List one way you could love God with your

    heart/mind

    soul/feelings

    strength/actions

11. Verse 7 tells parents to impress these commandments on their children. Rewrite this verse in your own words. A parent's job

67

12. Your parents may not write God's commands on your front gate, but try to think how they attempt to teach you to love and obey God by drawing a parallel to each of the ways mentioned in verses 7-9.

    Sit at home

    Walk along road

    Lie down

    Get up

    Symbols on hands/foreheads

    Symbols on doors/gates

13. What is your conclusion about a parent's job as seen in these verses? What does God expect parents to teach their children?

14. If children are to learn to obey God (whom they can't see), they must first learn to obey their parents (whom they can see). Can you now think of your parents as trainers of obedience to God?

    Yes   Not sure   No

Now look again at Colossians 3:20: "Children, obey your parents in everything, for this pleases the Lord." With this in mind, write below three ways in which you have rebelled in obeying your parents' rules. Looking at these three problem areas, what changes could you make in attempting to obey them?

   1.

   2.

   3.

LESSON 11

The Problem of Money

Genesis 3:17-19

1. If you were given $1000, what is the first thing you'd buy?

    Second?

    Absolute last thing you'd want to buy

    Would you save any?

2. Plan a budget for an allowance of $50 per month.

____ tapes/records

____ books

____ clothes

____ savings

____ toiletries/cosmetics

____ movies/entertainment

____ church

____ impulse spending

3. List below an example of wasteful use of money.

4. List a good cause to which you would give money.

5. List one advantage and one disadvantage of a society that doesn't use money.

Advantage   Disadvantage

6. Name anything you can think of that is more important than money.

Let's look at Genesis 3:17-19 to get a biblical perspective on work and money. These verses are God speaking to Adam after his sin of eating the fruit in the Garden of Eden.

---

17) To Adam he said, "Because you listened to your wife and ate from the tree about which I commanded you, 'You must not eat of it,'
"Cursed is the ground because of you;
   through painful toil you will eat of it all the days of your life.
18) It will produce thorns and thistles for you,
   and you will eat the plants of the field.
19) By the sweat of your brow
   will you eat your food
until you return to the ground,
   since from it you were taken;
for dust you are
   and to dust you will return."

Genesis 3:17-19

7. What was Adam's punishment for eating the fruit (v. 17)?

8. What does verse 18 say Adam will reap for his toil?

9. Describe Adam's work as depicted in verse 19.

10. Do you find any mention of reward (money) for Adam's labor?

    Yes   Indirectly   No

11. What do you think was God's purpose for Adam originally (before he sinned and his efforts were cursed to fail?)

12. How does the idea of working "for the joy of it" fit into our society?

Name the professions that you think people choose who are more interested in the work than in the money.

13. If people really did find their reward in doing their work well, how would this change our society?

14. How does this idea change your attitude toward the desire for money?
    ❑ makes me want to choose a career I'd enjoy
    ❑ helps me understand God's warning against love of money
    ❑ makes me wish we could do away with money altogether
    ❑ it doesn't change my thinking at all

15. How do you think our lives should be spent?
    ❑ working hard to earn a living
    ❑ enjoying our work as God intended
    ❑ seeking more money
    ❑ putting pursuit of money before God's will

16. Consider what is most important in your life.
    ❑ time or money   ❑ hobby or money
    ❑ pleasure or money   ❑ education or money
    ❑ family or money   ❑ love or money
    ❑ nature or money   ❑ freedom or money
    ❑ friends or money   ❑ God's will or money

LESSON 12

Fearing the Future

Isaiah 41

1. What do you see yourself doing ten years from now?
    ❑ College?
    ❑ Married?
    ❑ Children? How many?
    ❑ Job? What kind?
    ❑ Dead?
    ❑ Other?

2. When you think about the future, do you have an overall positive attitude or a negative one?

3. What scares you most about the future?
    ❑ Disease: cancer/AIDS?
    ❑ Responsibility? (explain)
    ❑ Marriage? What in particular
    ❑ Parenthood? What in particular
    ❑ Unemployment?
    ❑ Threat of nuclear war?
    ❑ Death?

4. What events in the future are you eagerly awaiting?

5. How often do you think about nuclear war?
    ❑ Once a year
    ❑ Once a month
    ❑ Once a week
    ❑ Once a day

6. Do you think God could stop the world from being destroyed? How?

What do your friends say about the future?

Death was not part of God's original plan. But that doesn't mean He isn't in control now. God always has a "Plan B." The Bible says five important things for us to remember about the end of the world.

> Lift up your eyes to the heavens:
>   Who created all these?
> He who brings out the starry host one by one,
>   and calls them each by name.
> Because of his great power and mighty strength,
>   not one of them is missing.
>
> *Isaiah 40:26*

7. *God is the creator of the universe.* What do you think He could do for you?

> He tends his flock like a shepherd:
>   He gathers the lambs in his arms
> and carries them close to his heart;
>   He gently leads those who have young.
>
> *Isaiah 40:11*

8. *God is the keeper of the universe.* What do you think are the "lambs" in this verse? How does a shepherd care for his lambs? What do you think God could do for you?

74

> He brings princes to naught
>   and reduces the rulers of this world to nothing.
>
> *Isaiah 40:23*

9. *God is the ruler of the universe.* Does this verse help you to believe in God's control of the world, even though you can't see it? (Yes/No)

10. List three "princes and rulers" (problems) you'd like God to "bring to naught" (solve) for you.

    1.

    2.

    3.

> 29) He gives strength to the weary
>   and increases the power of the weak.
> 30) Even youths grow tired and weary,
>   and young men stumble and fall;
> 31) but those who hope in the Lord
>   will renew their strength.
> They will soar on wings like eagles;
>   they will run and not grow weary,
>   they will walk and not be faint.
>
> *Isaiah 40:29-31*

11. *God is stronger than evil.* In what area of your life do you need strengthening so you can soar?

> 21) Do you not know?
>   Have you not heard?
> Has it not been told since the beginning?
>   Have you not understood since the earth was founded?
> 22) He sits enthroned above the circle of the earth,
>   and its people are like grasshoppers. . . .
>
> 28) Do you not know?
>   Have you not heard?
> The Lord is the everlasting God,
>   the Creator of the ends of the earth.
> He will not grow tired or weary,
>   and his understanding no one can fathom.
>
> *Isaiah 40:21, 22, 28*

12. *God will win in the end.* What do these verses offer that you need?

13. How has your thinking changed because of this lesson?

14. List your conclusions from reading Isaiah 40.

15. What do you think the Bible promises for *your* future?

16. What can you begin to do *today* with this future?

17. What can you tell your friends who are afraid?

LESSON 13

Daily Time Alone With God (D.T.A.W.G.)

Daniel 6

1. How do you spend your day? Estimate the amount of time you spend on the following activities in a day.

   _____ sleeping   _____ school day
   _____ eating   _____ sports
   _____ television   _____ friends
   _____ reading   _____ family, pet
   _____ daydreaming   _____ talking on the phone
   _____ reading the Bible   _____ praying

2. From what source does most of your thinking come?

   _____ friends   _____ family
   _____ television   _____ God

3. Why do you think reading the Bible and prayer receive so little attention in our day's activities?
   ❏ too busy
   ❏ don't understand it
   ❏ don't see any need for it
   ❏ too boring
   ❏ don't know how

4. What effects might Bible reading and prayer have on your life?

Let's look at a young man who found prayer helpful in his life.

> 7) The royal administrators, prefects, satraps, advisers and governors have all agreed that the king should issue an edict and enforce the decree that anyone who prays to any god or man during the next thirty days, except to you, O king, shall be thrown into the lions' den. 8) Now, O king, issue the decree and put it in writing so that it cannot be altered—in accordance with the laws of the Medes and Persians, which cannot be annulled. 9) So King Darius put the decree in writing.
>
> 10) Now when Daniel learned that the decree had been published, he went home to his upstairs room where the windows opened toward Jerusalem. Three times a day he got down on his knees and prayed, giving thanks to his God, just as he had done before.
>
> 25) Then King Darius wrote to all the peoples, nations and men of every language throughout the land:
> "May you prosper greatly!
> 26) "I issue a decree that in every part of my kingdom people must fear and reverence the God of Daniel.
>
> "For he is the living God
> and he endures forever;
> his kingdom will not be destroyed,
> his dominion will never end.
> 27) He rescues and he saves;
> he performs signs and wonders
> in the heavens and on the earth.
> He has rescued Daniel
> from the power of the lions."
>
> 28) So Daniel prospered during the reign of Darius and the reign of Cyrus the Persian.
>
> *Daniel 6:7-10, 25-28*

5. According to King Darius, what is God able to do?

6. What two answers to Daniel's prayer do we see in these verses?

7. Even Jesus prayed to God, His Father. Read Matthew 14:23: "After he dismissed them, he went up into the hills by himself to pray. When evening came, he was there alone." Why do you think Jesus would need to pray all night?
   ❑ lonely; wanted someone to talk to
   ❑ tired and bored
   ❑ didn't know God, His father, well enough
   ❑ got His strength from communicating with God

8. Describe the last time you felt weak, helpless, or in need of someone stronger to work out a problem for you.

Reading the Bible helps us to know that God loves us, wants to act in our lives like He did in Daniel's, and wants us to be like Him. David, who loved the Bible, wrote Psalm 119 about it.

> 9) How can a young man keep his way pure?
>   By living according to your word.
> 10) I seek you with all my heart;
>   do not let me stray from your commands.
> 11) I have hidden your word in my heart
>   that I might not sin against you.
> 12) Praise be to you, O Lord;
>   teach me your decrees.
> 13) With my lips I recount
>   all the laws that come from your mouth.
> 14) I rejoice in following your statutes
>   as one rejoices in great riches.
> 15) I meditate on your precepts
>   and consider your ways.
> 16) I delight in your decrees;
>   I will not neglect your word.
>
> *Psalm 119:9-16*

9. List the six different words David uses for biblical guidelines in these verses (some are used twice).

10. Now list what David does with God's Word (hint: look at the verbs in these verses).

   v. 9:

   v. 10:

   v. 11:

   v. 12:

   v. 13:

   v. 14:

   v. 15:

   v. 16:

11. David truly seems to enjoy applying God's Word to his life. How can you do that? Read the following guidelines and fill in the blanks, adapting them to your life:

Time: Choose a time of day convenient for your D.T.A.W.G.

Place: Choose a place of privacy to meet regularly with God:

How to use this time:

   1. Bible reading: I will read the book of _____ first. (Reading through the New Testament is a good way to begin.)
   2. Devotional books/studies: I will follow _____ for devotional reading.
   3. Prayer: I will pray _____ minutes each day.
   4. Prayer journal: I will pray for

Family/friends   Church needs

World needs   My own needs

(Be sure to date the request and answer to prayer.)

Prayer Journal: 1. Family 2. Friends 3. Church 4. World 5. Me 6. And much more...